Silver Burdett Ginn Science

DISCOVERYWORKS

Silver Burdett Ginn

Parsippany, NJ   Needham, MA

Atlanta, GA   Deerfield, IL   Irving, TX   Santa Clara, CA

Authors

William Badders
Science Resource Teacher
Cleveland Public Schools
Cleveland, OH

Lowell J. Bethel
Professor of Science Education
The University of Texas at Austin
Austin, TX

Victoria Fu
Professor of Child Development
Virginia Polytechnic Institute and
State University
Blacksburg, VA

Donald Peck
Director, Center for Elementary Science
Fairleigh Dickinson University
Madison, NJ

Carolyn Sumners
Director of Astronomy and Physics
Houston Museum of Natural Science
Houston, TX

Catherine Valentino
Senior Vice President for
Curriculum Development
Voyager Expanded Learning
West Kingston, RI

Consulting Author

R. Mike Mullane
Astronaut, retired
Albuquerque, NM

Contributing Writers

Wendy Pfeffer
Jeanne Gleason

Credits and acknowledgements appear on page H15,
which consistutes an extension of this copyright page.

Silver Burdett Ginn
A Division of Simon & Schuster
299 Jefferson Road, P.O. Box 480
Parsippany, NJ 07054-0480

ISBN 0-382-38857-7

2 3 4 5 6 7 8 9 10 RRD 05 04 03 02 01 00 99 98 97 96

CONTENTS

UNIT A

INTERACTIONS OF LIVING THINGS

Themes: Constancy and Change, Models

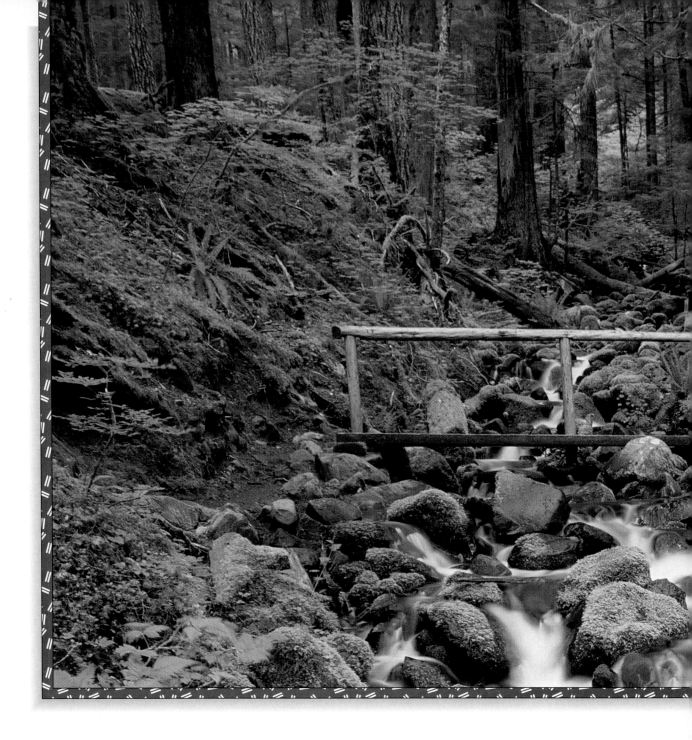

Living and Nonliving Things

Imagine being in this woodland. How might you classify the things around you? You could classify them as living, once-living, or nonliving things.

A **living thing** needs food, water, and air. It can grow. A living thing can also make new living things. The trees and other plants are living things.

Once-living things are not living now. They were living in the past. What things in the picture were once living? Dead leaves, the logs of the bridge, and broken twigs are once-living things.

Nonliving things have never needed food, water, or air. They have not grown. They have not made new living things. Rocks and soil are nonliving things.

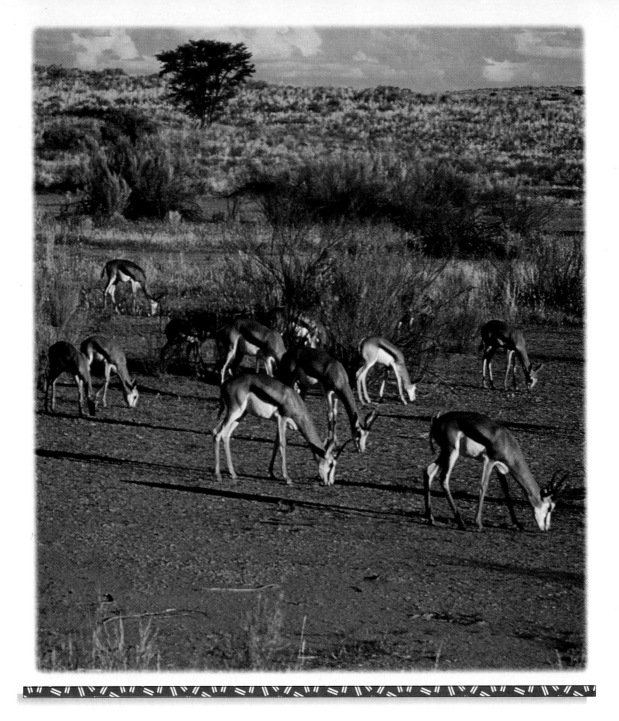

Living Things Have Needs

A **habitat** is the home of a living thing. In a habitat, plants and animals get what they need to live.

The first picture shows a desert habitat. There is food, air, and light for the living things. There is not much water. Desert plants and animals can live where there is little water.

INTERACTIONS OF LIVING THINGS

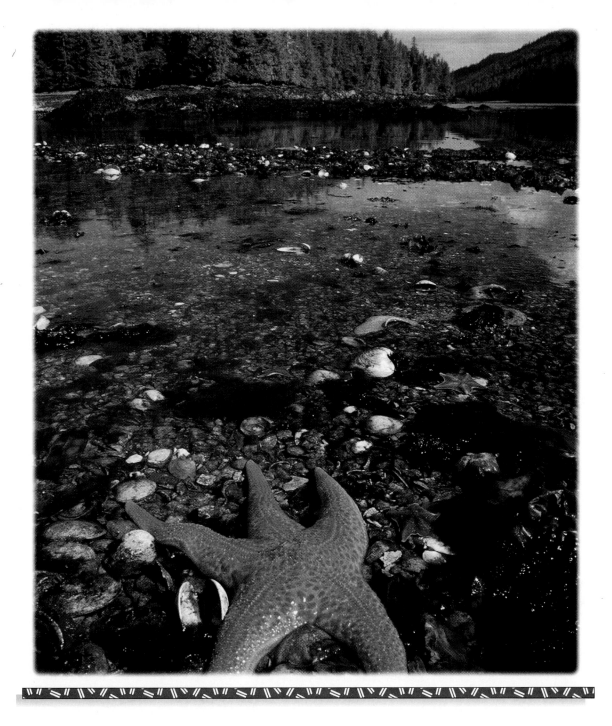

The second picture shows a seacoast habitat. It also has food, air, and light. The seacoast has a lot of water. It is salty water. Some plants and animals make their homes in the sea. They need salty water to live.

The picture shows colorful sea stars. A sea star is an animal that eats other animals. The sea star gets what it needs from its seacoast habitat.

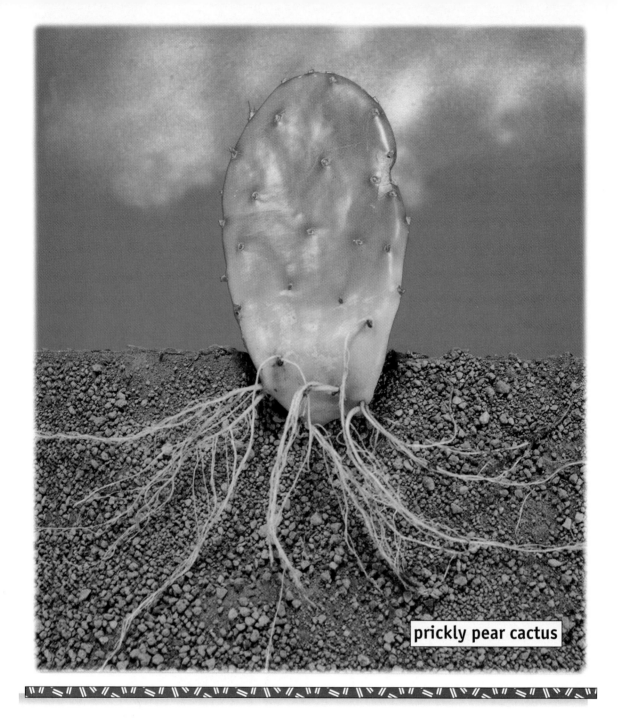

prickly pear cactus

All About Plants

What parts do both of these plants have? They both have roots. **Roots** help hold each plant in the soil. Roots also take in water and minerals from the soil.

Both plants have stems. **Stems** carry water and food to other parts of the plant. The stem in a cactus also makes food and stores water.

INTERACTIONS OF LIVING THINGS

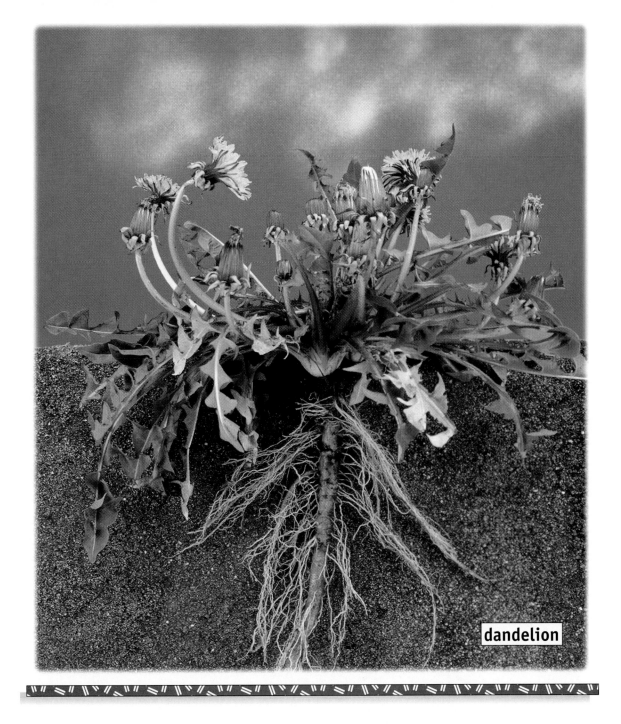

dandelion

Leaves make food for a plant. Different plants have different kinds of leaves. The dandelion has broad, flat leaves. The cactus has tiny, sharp leaves called **spines.** Spines help protect the cactus by keeping animals from eating it. Plants lose less water from spines than from broad, flat leaves. Turn the page to see these parts labeled.

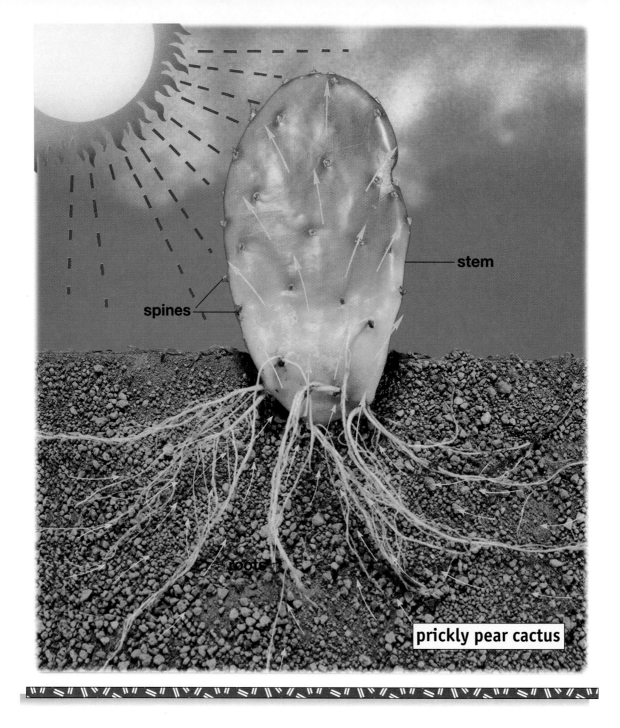

spines

stem

roots

prickly pear cactus

How does a plant get what it needs to live? Point to the roots, stem, and spines of the cactus. Follow the blue arrows up from the roots. The arrows show how water moves through a cactus.

Look at the dandelion. Water and minerals move from the roots to the stems to the leaves. This is how the plants get what they need.

INTERACTIONS OF LIVING THINGS

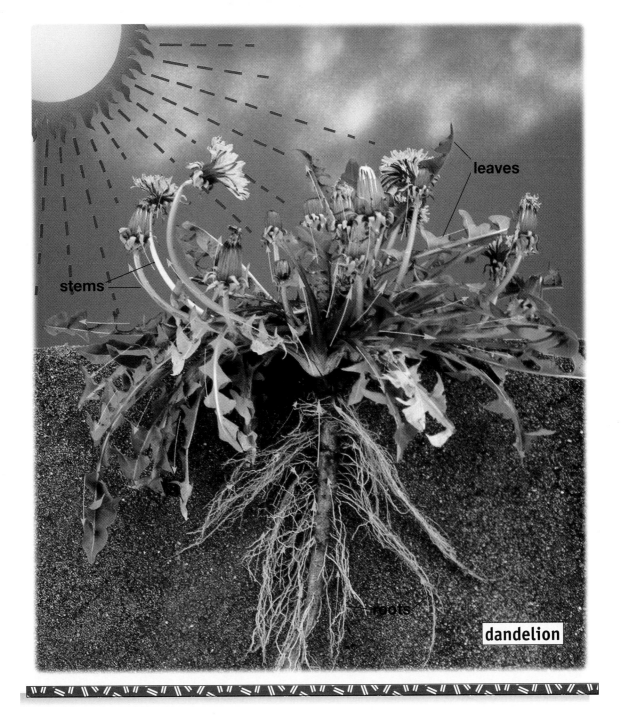

leaves

stems

roots

dandelion

The roots of these plants are different. The cactus lives in the desert. Its roots stay near the top of the soil. This helps them take in water quickly when rain falls.

Plants need more than food, water, and air to live. They also need light. The plants in the picture are getting light from the sun. Plants use sunlight to help them make food.

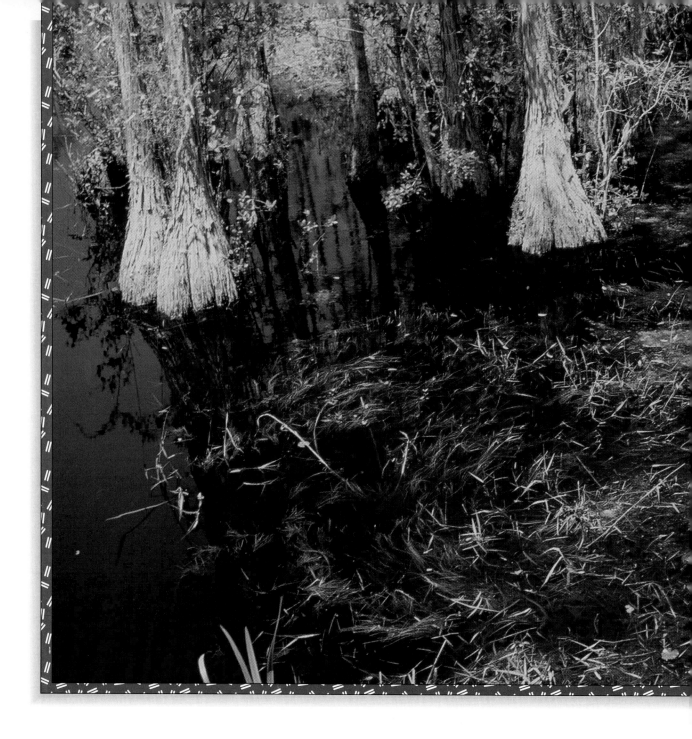

Meeting Needs

A swamp is a habitat. Many plants and animals live in a swamp. Water covers the land in a swamp most of the time.

Look at the picture. You can see water, trees, grasses, and an alligator. Birds also live in swamps. How is a swamp different from a desert or a woodland?

INTERACTIONS OF LIVING THINGS

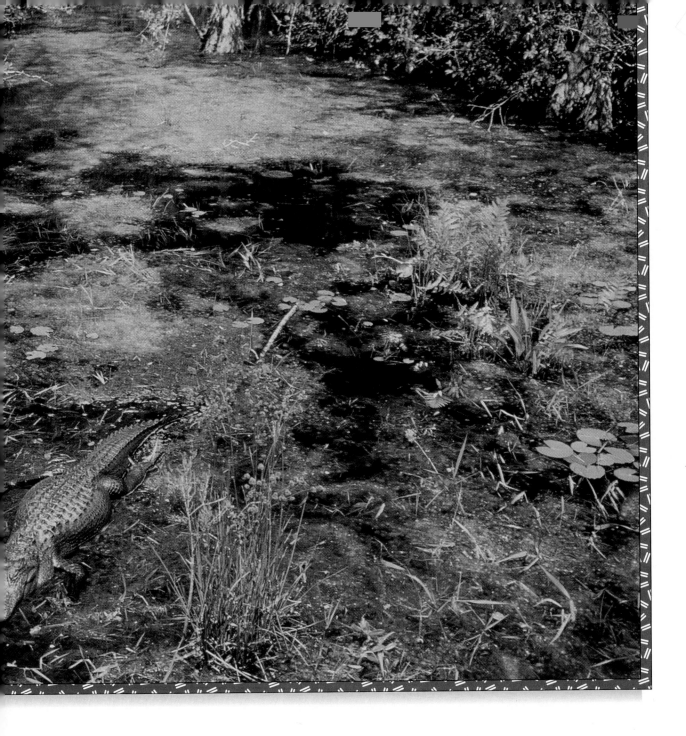

Things that plants and animals use to live are called **resources.** The alligator uses living things in the swamp for food. It eats frogs, birds, and other animals.

The alligator also uses nonliving things to live. These things include air, light, and water. Look again at the picture. What other things in the swamp might an animal use to live?

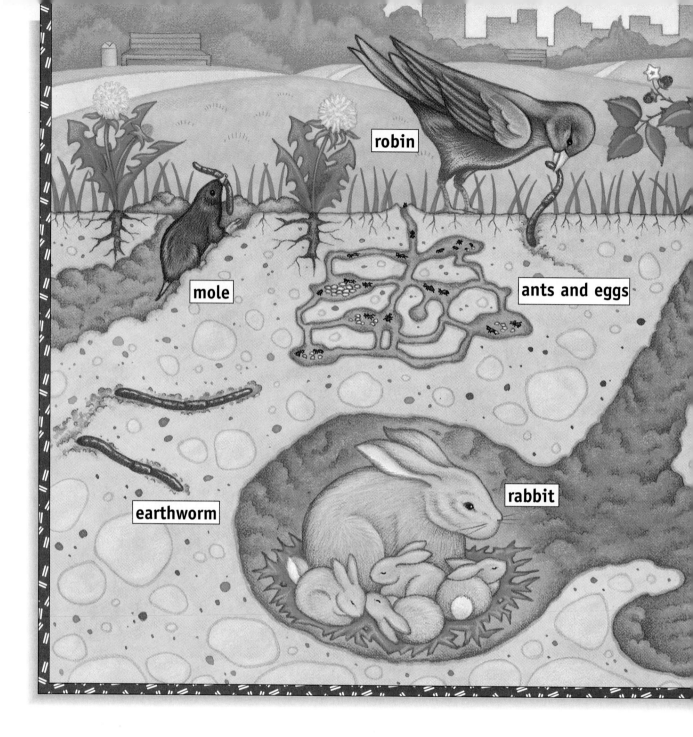

robin

mole

ants and eggs

earthworm

rabbit

Underground Homes

All animals need a shelter. A **shelter** is a place where an animal can rest and be safe. It protects the animal from heat and cold. It is a place to store food. It is also a place to take care of young.

Shelters can be made with living and nonliving things. Shelters can be in many places.

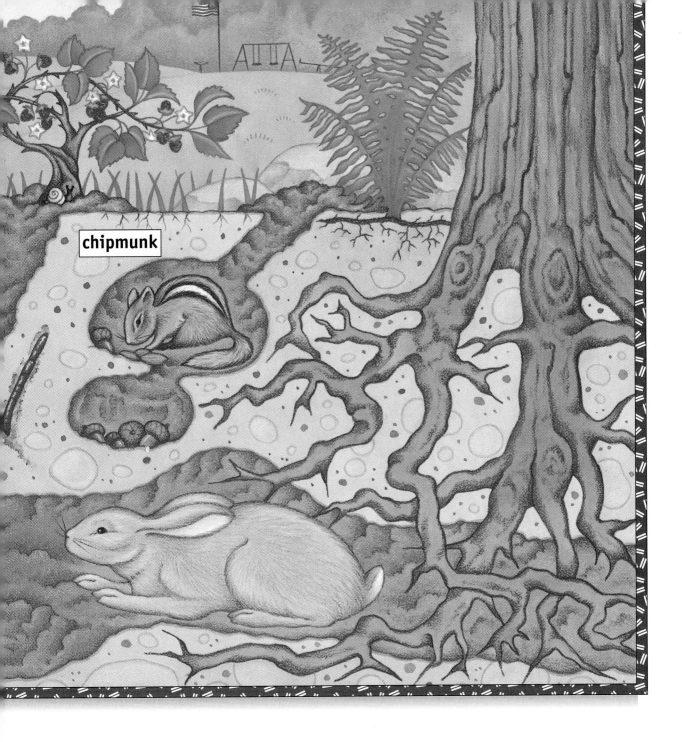

chipmunk

Look at the picture. Some of the animals make their homes underground. The mother rabbit puts grass in her shelter. She makes a soft nest for her young.

The chipmunk stores acorns in its shelter. The ants lay their eggs in tunnels. The earthworms find food in the soil. All these animals made their homes by digging into the soil.

toco toucan

downy woodpecker

Getting Food

Animals have body parts that help them live. A **beak** is a mouth part that helps a bird get food.

Some birds have beaks that are used to pick up tiny things like seeds or nuts. The toucan carries eggs in its beak. The woodpecker uses its beak to drill through nuts and bark to get food.

common moorhen

northern shoveler drake

Atlantic puffin

ibis

The long beak of the ibis is used to spear fish or
frogs in shallow water. The puffin's beak is good for
gobbling up many small fish.

Some birds have scooping beaks that are also called
bills. The moorhen and the drake are birds that live in
water. They eat plants. They use their bills to scoop
plants out of the water.

Changing the Habitat

Some animals make changes to the place in which they live. A beaver is one such animal. It uses its teeth to cut down trees. Look at the tree that the beaver is cutting. The cut tree will fall in the river. This is the beginning of a beaver dam. The beaver dam will cross the riverbed from one side to the other.

INTERACTIONS OF LIVING THINGS

The three small photos show a beaver at work. The beaver uses its sharp teeth to cut down trees. As it swims, it carries twigs in its mouth. It uses its legs, feet, and tail to swim. Its paddle-shaped tail helps it pack twigs, stones, and mud around the trees.

Turn the page. See how the woodland looks after the beaver builds its dam.

The beaver has built the dam. A pond has formed behind it. The pond is a place of still water. Here the beaver builds its shelter.

The beaver's shelter is called a **lodge.** It is made of the same things the beaver used for the dam—trees, twigs, mud, and stones. A beaver stays warm, stores food, and raises its young in a lodge.

The beaver changes the woodland in many ways. When the beaver cuts down trees, animals that lived in those trees lose their homes. Animals that eat parts of trees, such as fruit or leaves, lose their food.

The pond that forms behind the dam floods some of the land. Animals that lived on that land need to find new homes.

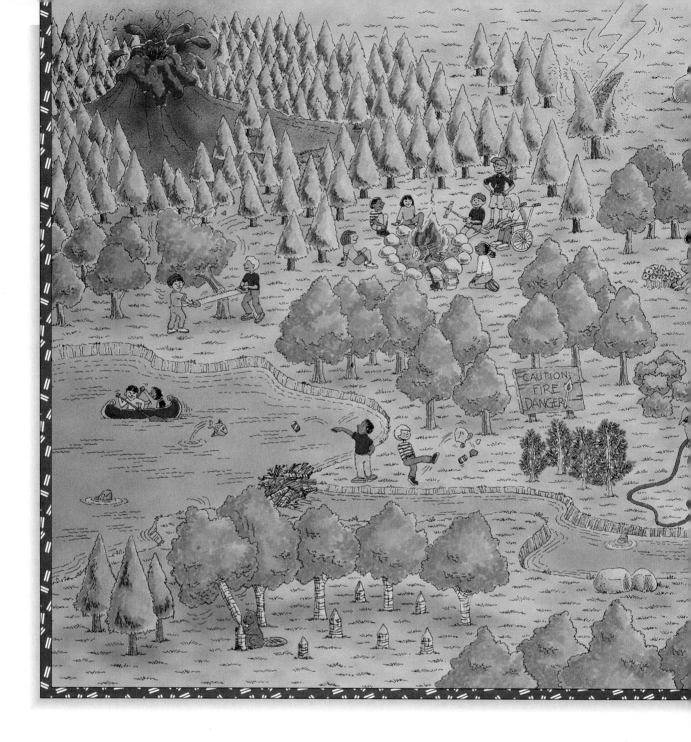

More Changes

People can change an area. Natural forces can also change an area. Changes can be both helpful and harmful. Look at the picture. In what ways are people helping and harming this area?

Planting trees and picking up trash are helpful. Building a road or a house can harm an area.

Cutting down trees can cause erosion. **Erosion** is the washing away of land. The roots of trees can help stop erosion. Roots hold soil in place.

Forest fires can be helpful or harmful. They are helpful when they clear away twigs, leaves, and dead trees. Forest fires are harmful when they kill living things.

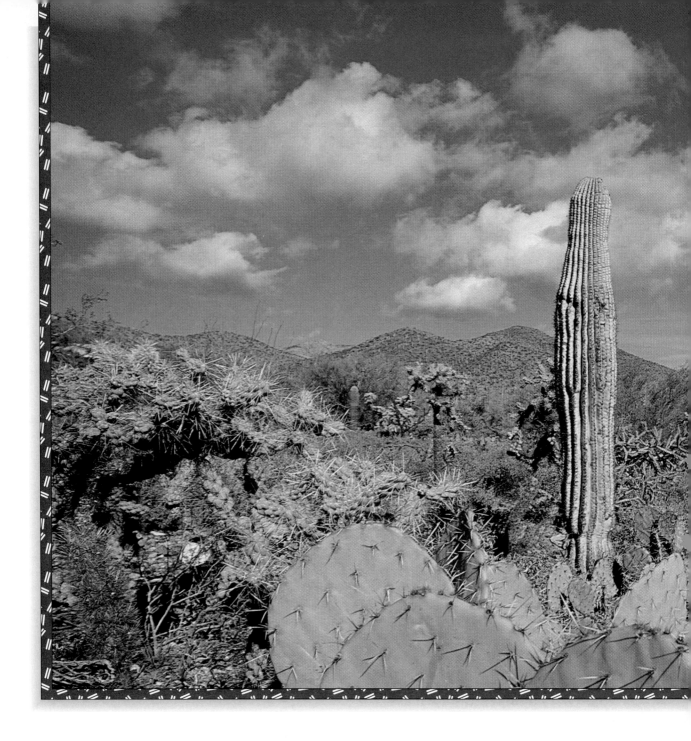

Living in the Desert

A desert is a place that gets very little rain. There are many kinds of living things in this desert. What kinds of living things do you see?

Many of the plants in this picture are cactuses. Like other plants, they are green and have stems and roots. How are cactuses different from other plants?

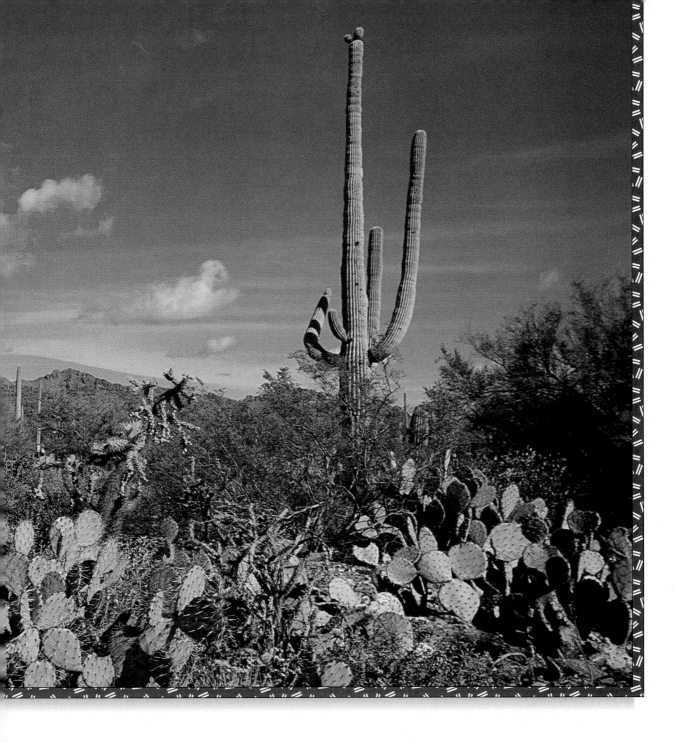

Desert plants and animals need the same things as other plants and animals. They need food, water, air, and light.

Desert plants and animals can live where the days are very hot and the nights are cold. They can also live with very little water. What plants and animals could not stay alive in the desert?

Some Other Habitats

These two animals live in different places. The polar bear lives where it is cold and snowy. The flamingo lives where it is warm and wet.

What helps a polar bear live in the Arctic? It has thick fur that helps keep it warm. Its fur is white. This color helps a polar bear hide on ice and snow.

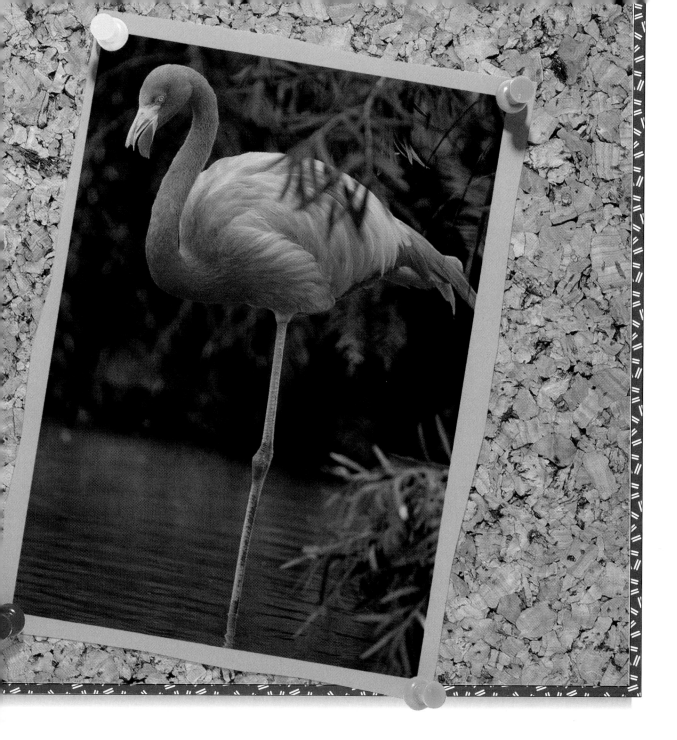

What helps a flamingo live in wet places? Its long
legs help it wade in water to find food. Its bill helps it
scoop food out of the water. This bird also uses its bill
to scoop mud as it builds a nest.

Polar bears and flamingos cannot live in the desert.
A desert would be too warm and dry for a polar bear. It
would be too dry for a flamingo.

Word Power

A. Match the words with a picture.
living thing   once-living thing   nonliving thing

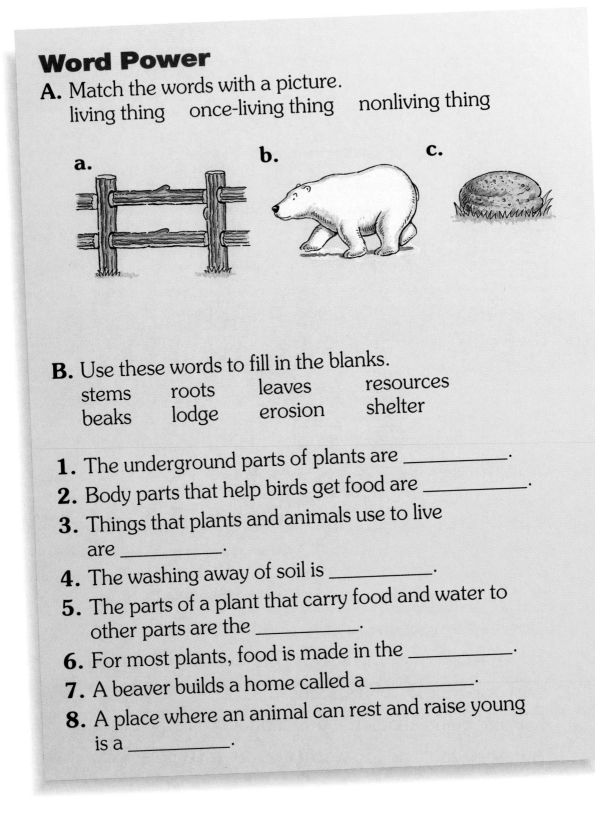

a.   b.   c.

B. Use these words to fill in the blanks.
stems   roots   leaves   resources
beaks   lodge   erosion   shelter

1. The underground parts of plants are _____.

2. Body parts that help birds get food are _____.

3. Things that plants and animals use to live
are _____.

4. The washing away of soil is _____.

5. The parts of a plant that carry food and water to
other parts are the _____.

6. For most plants, food is made in the _____.

7. A beaver builds a home called a _____.

8. A place where an animal can rest and raise young
is a _____.

Using Science Ideas

How many living things can you find in this woodland habitat? List them.

Solving Science Problems

1. Why do living things need food, water, air, and light?

2. Why can't a polar bear live in the desert?

3. Make a chart like the one shown. Add more living things. Then complete your chart.

Living Thing	Habitat	Special Features
polar bear	Arctic	thick fur

UNIT B

LIGHT AND COLOR

Theme: Systems

Looking for Light

Many things in this picture give off **light.** Some are made by people. Others are natural. Which things that give off light are natural? The stars in the sky are natural things that give off light. The burning logs are also natural things that give off light. Our most important source of light is not in this picture.

The sun is our most important source of light. It makes life on the earth possible. Other natural things that give off light are lightning and fireflies.

Electric bulbs give off light and are made by people. Oil lamps and gaslights also give off light. They too are made by people. What other things that give off light are made by people?

Lighting Up the Night

Some animals, such as owls and cats, can see well when there is very little light. People need more light to see well.

In the picture above, the room is dark. The boy can't see clearly. Things look different to him than they really are. He thinks animals are in the room.

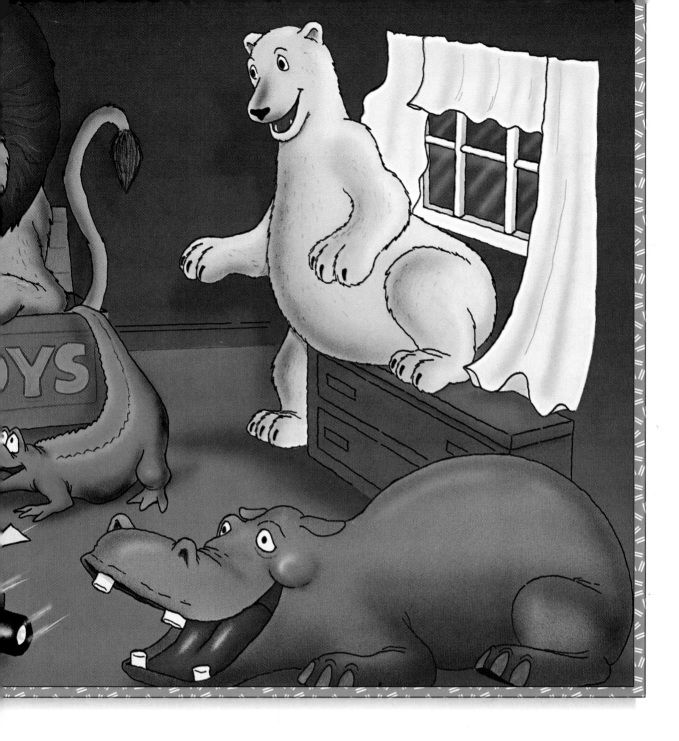

If you look outdoors in the dark, you might imagine you see something that really isn't there. At night, a few trees might look like a jungle. A fire hydrant might look like a monkey.

When you look outdoors during the day, things look different. Turn the page to see what the boy's room looks like in the light.

Light helps the boy see what's really there. There are no animals in the room.

When do you use light? You might use a lamp to help you read at night. You might use a flashlight to brighten a dark path. You might use a nightlight to light up a hallway at night.

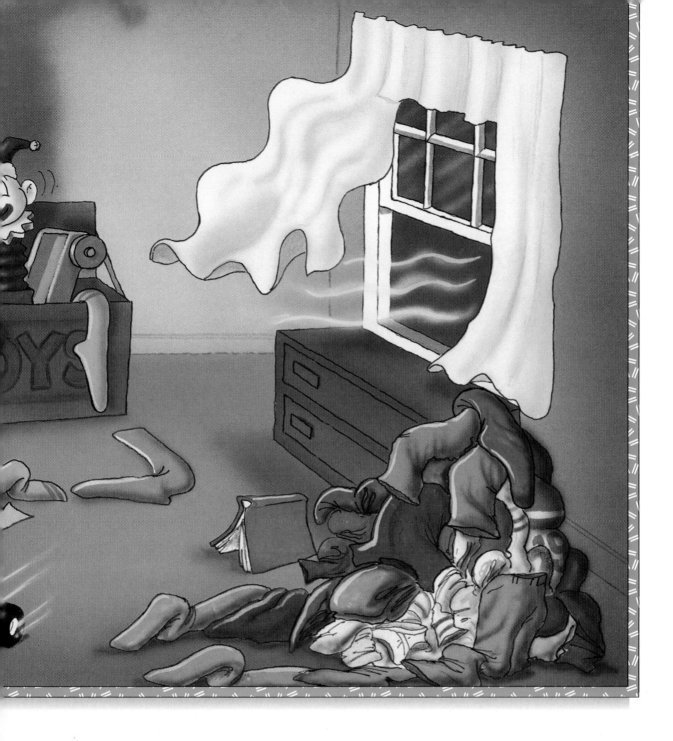

The moon can help you see at night. It does not give off its own light. The moon **reflects** sunlight. That means sunlight hits the moon and bounces off it.

Light can help keep people safe. Streetlights brighten the sidewalks for people who are walking. Bike reflectors help drivers see riders at night.

Light and Heat

Imagine sitting by a campfire like the one in the picture. How would you feel? You would feel warm. The fire provides both light and **heat.** What other objects in the picture give off light and heat? The flashlight, the lantern, and the stars all give off light and heat. Some objects give off more light and heat than others.

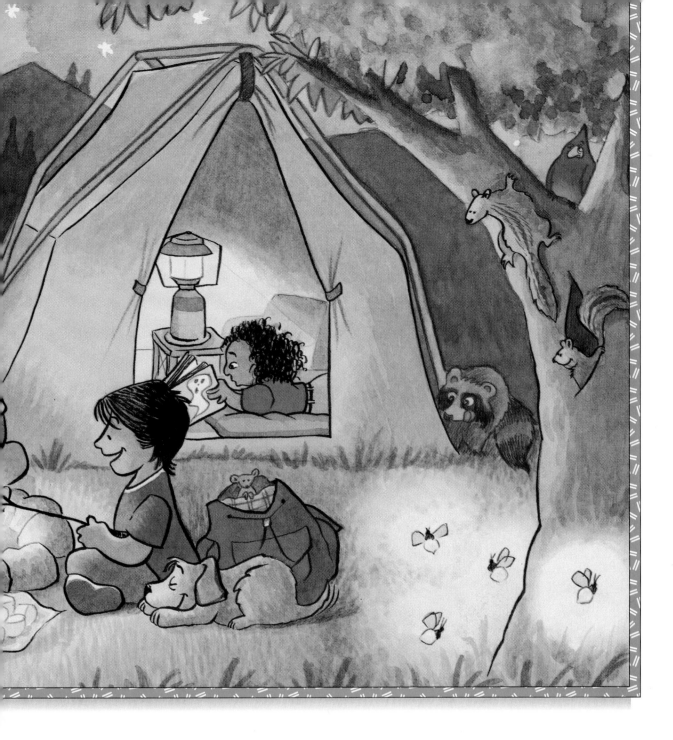

The closer you are to a light source, the more heat you feel. Most stars are very far away. You do not feel their heat. One star is close enough for you to feel its heat. That star is the sun. The sun lights and heats the earth's air, land, and water.

Which people in the picture feel the most heat from the campfire? Which people feel the least?

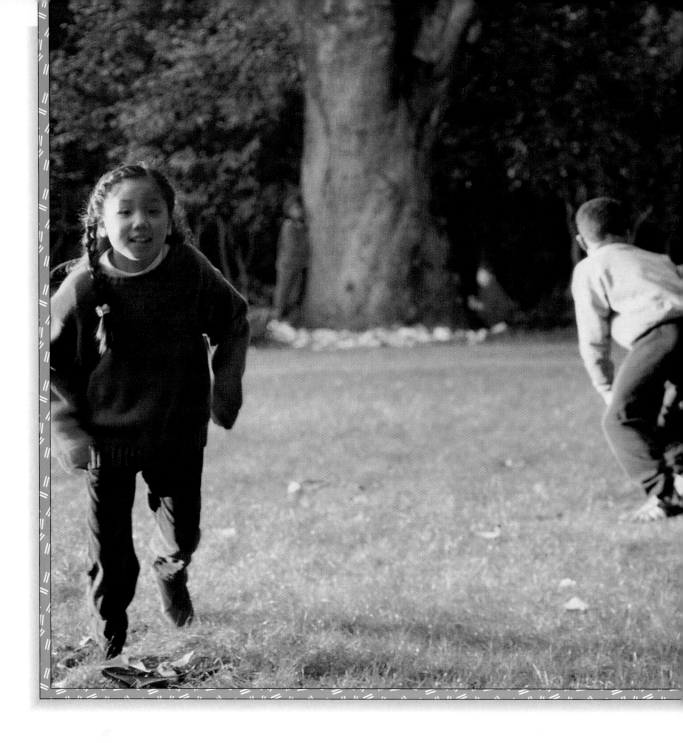

Beams of Light

What fun it is to play hide-and-seek! In this game, the person who is "it" must shine a flashlight on each child. Think about how light travels. Where might you hide so you won't get caught? You might hide behind a tree. The tree would block the **beam** of light. Why does the tree block the light?

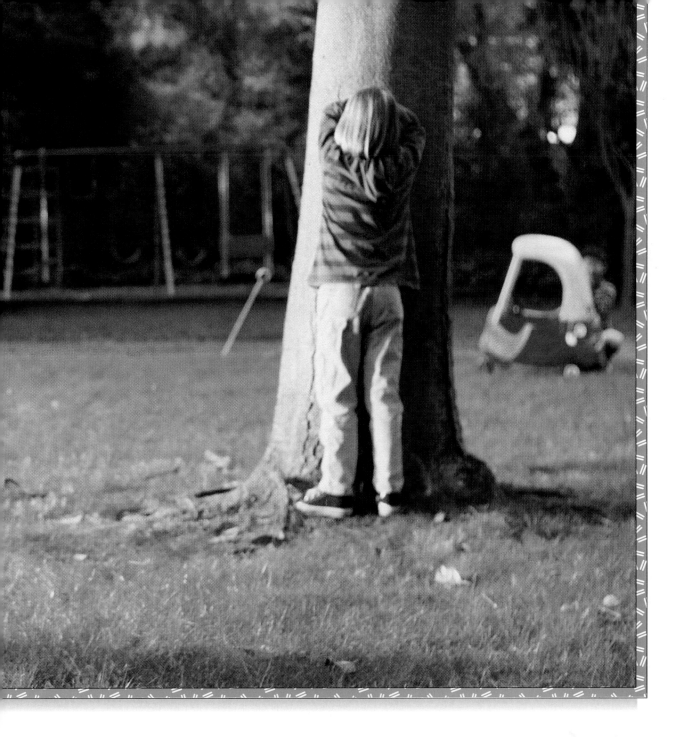

Light travels in **straight** lines. That's why the tree blocks the beam of light. Light does not curve around an object, such as a tree or a play car.

How does light get from an electric light bulb to a book? Beams of light travel out from the bulb in all directions. Each beam travels in a straight line. Some beams shine on the pages of the book.

Can You See the Light?

Light passes through some objects. Those objects are **transparent.** Some objects let a little light through. They are **translucent.** Others let no light pass through. Those objects are **opaque.**

This picture has three coverings. Which one is opaque? Which is transparent? Which is translucent?

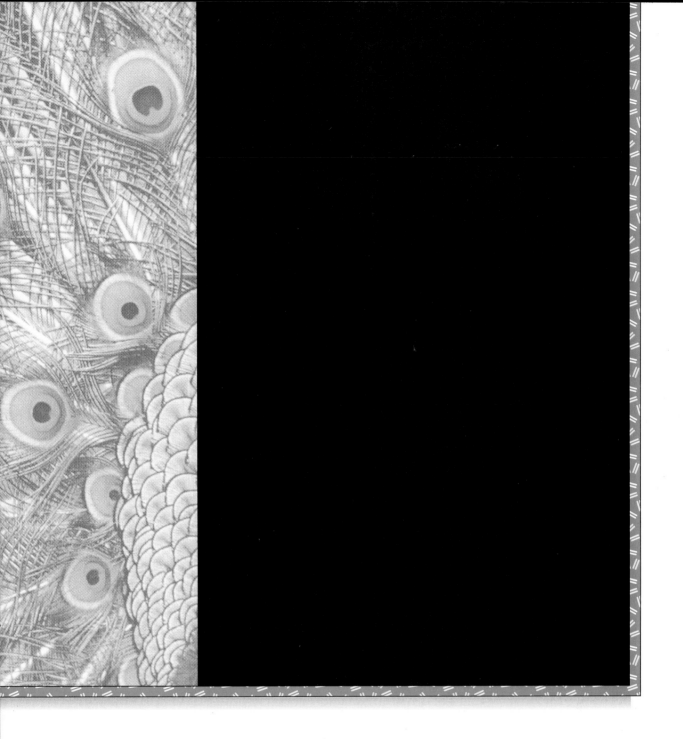

Pretend you're at a friend's party. Everyone takes home a piece of cake. Your friend wraps the cake in waxed paper. How clearly can you see the cake? The cake looks blurred because waxed paper is translucent.

Think of a wrap that is opaque. You might suggest aluminum foil or brown paper. What kind of wrap is transparent?

Look at the picture now. The coverings have been removed. You can clearly see what was under the opaque and translucent coverings.

The transparent covering is clear. When it covered the picture, you could still see what was under it. What other things are transparent? You might think of a window or clear water.

Suppose you are sitting at your desk and sunlight is shining in your eyes. You hold up a piece of writing paper to block the sun. Some sunlight comes through the paper. The paper is translucent.

You then hold up a book. No sunlight comes through the book. That's because the book blocks the sunlight. The book is opaque.

Making Shadows

The picture shows shadow animals. They are made by shining a light on an opaque object. The object blocks the light and makes a **shadow.**

You can make shadows, too. In a dark room, stand in front of a light. Face away from the light. Look at your shadow on the wall.

SHADOW ZOO

Can you make your shadow move? Wiggle your arms. Shake your head. How does your shadow change?

Now look at your hand. It blocks the light. That's because your hand is opaque. It makes a shadow on the wall. Turn the page to find out how to use your hands to make shadow animals.

The shadow of two hands spread out makes a butterfly or bird. The shadow of one hand on top of another looks like an elephant. Can you see its trunk?

The alligator is the shadow of the palms of two hands held together. The shadow of an arm and hand makes a swan. What shadows can you make?

LIGHT AND COLOR

SHADOW ZOO

Try making a bunny shadow. Make a fist with one hand. Point two fingers to make the ears. How can you make your bunny shadow hop?

A shadow is made when a light shines on an opaque object. Look for shadows outdoors and indoors. You'll find them all around you when the light is right.

Shadows Can Change

Shadow length depends on where the light is. The light could be to one side of an opaque object. It could be near or far, high or low.

The first picture was taken in the morning. The sun is low in the sky. A low light makes a long shadow.

Look at the second picture. Imagine it's noontime, when the sun is high in the sky. Will the shadows be longer than in the morning, or shorter? When light comes from high up, objects make short shadows.

Later in the day the sun will be low in the sky. Then shadows will be long again.

Making Rainbows

It has just finished raining. The sun is shining through the clouds. Look at the sky. You see lines of different colors. These lines of colors are called a **rainbow.** The colors of a rainbow are red, orange, yellow, green, blue, indigo, and violet.

LIGHT AND COLOR

When it rains, drops of water in the air act like prisms. A **prism** is clear glass or plastic that is shaped like a pyramid.

White light passing through a prism bends. Sunlight passing through drops of water also bends. This light splits into the colors of the rainbow.

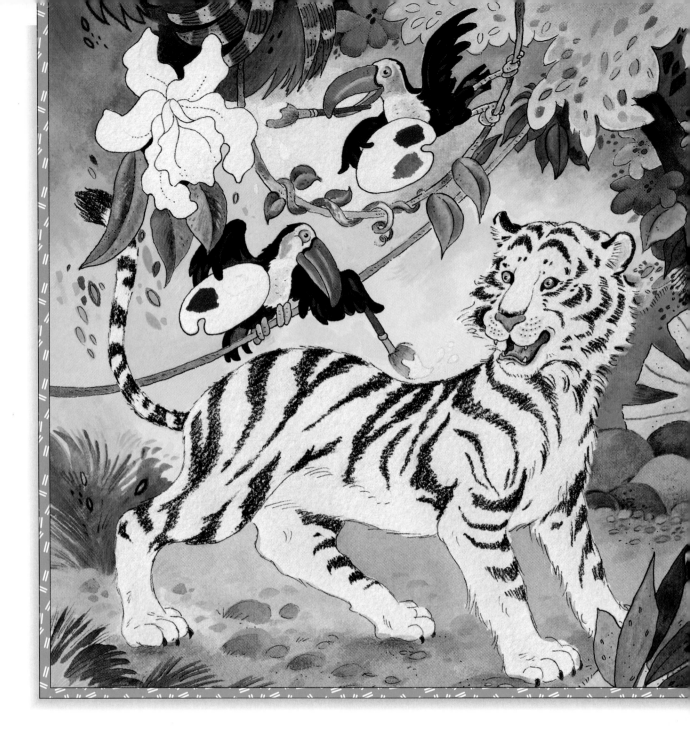

Making New Colors

Color is missing from parts of this picture. Colors can help us tell what things are.

The many colors on this page were made by mixing red, yellow, and blue. By mixing these colors you can make all the other colors.

The toucans are going to add the missing colors to this page. One toucan has red paint and blue paint. Another has red paint and yellow paint. What colors do the other toucans have?

When the toucans mix their paints, what colors will they get? If you turn the page, you'll find out.

The toucan that mixed red and blue paints made purple paint. He painted the flower. Find the toucan that mixed yellow and red. He painted the tiger orange. What colors were mixed to paint the snake? Blue and yellow were mixed to make green.

The monkey was painted brown. What colors were mixed to make brown?

LIGHT AND COLOR

How can you know which colors of paint to mix? The order of colors in the rainbow can help you. Orange is between red and yellow. You make orange paint by mixing red and yellow. Green is between yellow and blue in the rainbow. What colors should you mix to make green? What colors would you mix to make purple?

Word Power

A. Match the words with a picture.

transparent   translucent   opaque

a.

b.

c.

B. Use these words to fill in the blanks.

beam   light   reflects   prism
straight   shadow   heat   rainbow

1. The sun is our most important source of _____.
2. When drops of water in the sky break sunlight into different colors, a _____ forms.
3. When an object blocks light, you get a _____.
4. Light travels in a _____ line.
5. Stars give off both light and _____.
6. The moon _____ the light of the sun.
7. A flashlight sends out a _____ of light.
8. A _____ splits white light into colors.

Using Science Ideas

Explain where the light source is in each picture. What clues help you know the location of the light source?

a.

b.

Solving Science Problems

1. If the lights go out at night, what natural sources of light could you use?

2. Explain how white light splits into colors and what the order of the colors is.

3. Make a chart like the one shown. Fill in the colors you would get.

Colors you mix	Color you get
red and yellow	
red and blue	
yellow and blue	

EARTH THROUGH TIME

Themes: Models, Scale, Constancy and Change

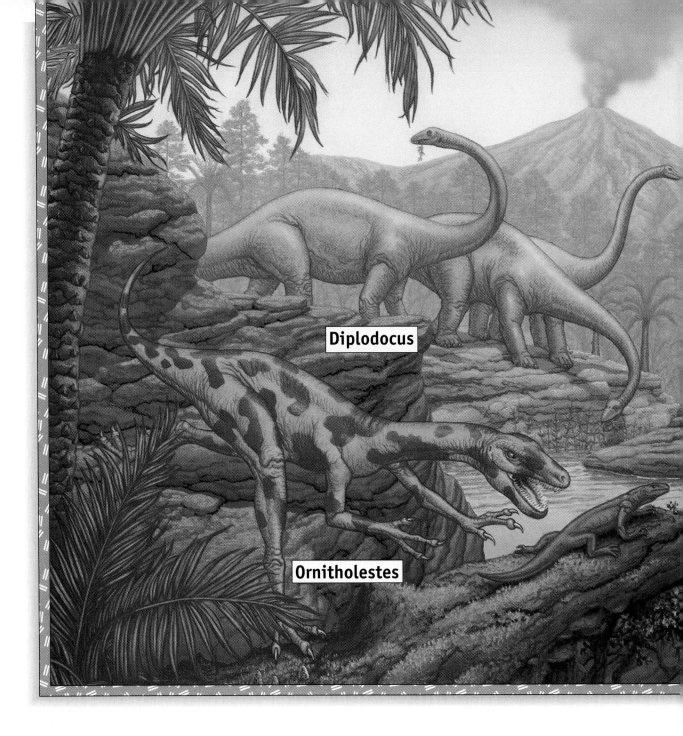

Diplodocus

Ornitholestes

All About Dinosaurs

Millions of years ago, **dinosaurs** lived on the earth. There were many kinds. Allosaurus had a big 36-inch (91-centimeter) head. Ornitholestes had a small 6-inch (15-centimeter) head. All dinosaurs had four limbs. Brachiosaurus walked on all four legs. Its front legs were longer than its back legs.

Brachiosaurus

Allosaurus

Allosaurus walked on two legs. Its front limbs were shorter. They had sharp claws. The front limbs were used to grab and hold food.

Different dinosaurs ate different kinds of foods. Diplodocus ate plants. Allosaurus ate other dinosaurs. Ornitholestes also ate meat. Dinosaurs were like each other. Yet they were different in many ways.

Lambeosaurus

Dinosaur Sizes

Dinosaurs were many sizes. This picture compares them to things we know today. Find Lambeosaurus. It's about 50 feet (15 meters) long. That's longer than a boxcar! Now find Triceratops. It's 30 feet (9 meters) long. That's as long as a school bus! Look at the size of Velociraptor. It's only 8 feet (2.4 meters) long.

Triceratops

Velociraptor

There were dinosaurs bigger and smaller than these. The smallest, Compsognathus, was the size of a chicken. It was about 30 inches (76 centimeters) long.

Seismosaurus was the longest at 170 feet (51 meters). That's twice as long as a basketball court! The largest, Brachiosaurus, weighed 40 tons (36 metric tons). That's as much as 10 hippopotamuses.

All About Fossils

Fossils are the remains or imprints of once-living things. **Remains** are parts of the living thing.

Find the remains in the picture. The bones are remains. They are from a mammoth. Scientists use these remains. They build models of animals with them. Models show what each animal looked like.

Find the imprints in the picture. There's a fish imprint. It shows the exact size and shape of the fish.

Fossil imprints work like rubber stamps. When you press an inked stamp on paper, you get an imprint. A leaf pressed in mud leaves an imprint, too. Imprints of dinosaur skin have been found. They show what dinosaur skin looked like.

Fossil Imprints

Fossil imprints form in mud or other matter that later hardens. Imagine the earth many years ago. A dinosaur walked on soft ground. Footprints were left. They turned to stone. Years later they're found. The footprints give clues about the size of the dinosaur and the shape of its feet.

Remains of plants can also become fossil imprints. Millions of years ago, leaves began to rot in a swamp. The leaves were covered by dirt. The pressure of the dirt changed the leaves to peat. More pressure turned the peat to coal. Leaf imprints were found in the coal. They show what the plants from many years ago looked like.

Fossil Footprints

Scientists study fossil footprints. The footprints are clues to how big dinosaurs were.

Look at the footprints above. What can help you match each footprint to the dinosaur that made it? You might look at the size of the footprint. You might look at the shape of the foot. You might count the toes.

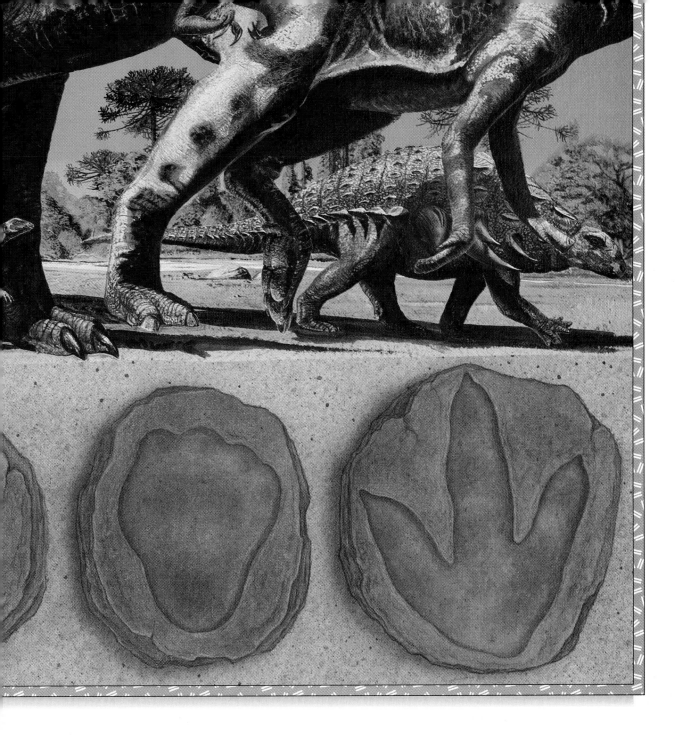

Imagine you are walking in the woods. You find small footprints. What can you tell about the animal that made those footprints? You might guess it was a very small animal.

Scientists compare footprints. In the same soil, the heavier animal left the deeper imprint. In harder soils, that same animal might leave shallow prints.

Stenonychosaurus

Ankylosaurus

Things Fossils Tell Us

Dinosaurs like these died long ago. Mud covered them. The soft parts of their bodies rotted. Only their bones remained. Years passed. The bones turned to stone. Later, scientists dug up the **fossil remains.** Scientists recreated the dinosaurs with these bones.

Ouranosaurus

Bones tell how long a dinosaur's legs were. They show the shape of its head. They even let us know what its neck looked like.

Look at the large bones. They belong to the large dinosaur. The small bones belong to the small dinosaur. By fitting bones together, scientists can tell how a dinosaur stood and walked.

Dinosaur Teeth

Look at the mouths of the dinosaurs. Point to their teeth. Look at the dinosaur in the back. Why can't you see its teeth? They are too far back in its mouth.

Which dinosaur will eat the plant? It needs blunt, **flat teeth** to grind the food. Which will eat the lizard? It needs sharp, **pointed teeth** to tear the food.

Scientists can tell what foods some dinosaurs ate. They look at the shape and sharpness of the teeth.

Most plant-eating dinosaurs had blunt, flat teeth to crush the plants. Most meat eaters had sharp, pointed teeth to tear the meat. Some dinosaurs had 2,000 teeth in their mouth. Turn the page to see the teeth of the dinosaurs in the picture.

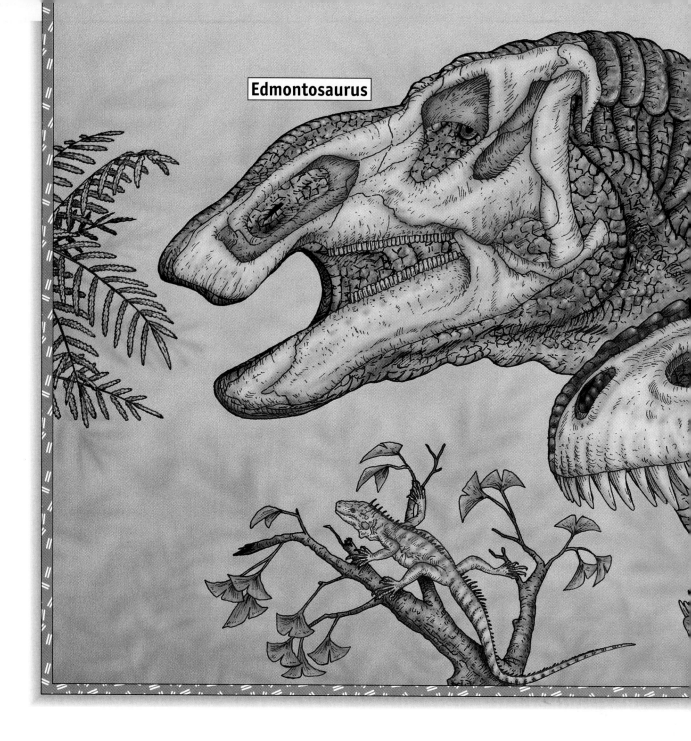

Edmontosaurus

This picture shows the skulls of the dinosaurs. The **skulls** show the teeth. Edmontosaurus had blunt, flat teeth. Its teeth were good for grinding food. It was a plant eater.

Albertosaurus's long jaw had many pointed teeth. The teeth were sharp like a knife for cutting meat. Albertosaurus was a meat eater.

Albertosaurus

Most people know about Tyrannosaurus. It had teeth that were 6 inches (15 centimeters) long. They were pointed like knives. The teeth had edges like a saw. What do you think Tyrannosaurus ate?

Some toothless dinosaurs had bills. They used their bills to catch worms, insects, and soft lizards. Other toothless dinosaurs ate plants.

Looking at Skeletons

Think about putting together a puzzle. Dinosaur bones are like pieces of a puzzle. Scientists find a few dinosaur bones at a time. They put the bones together to make a **skeleton.** Scientists use real bones to build skeletons. The model then is the exact size and shape of the dinosaur.

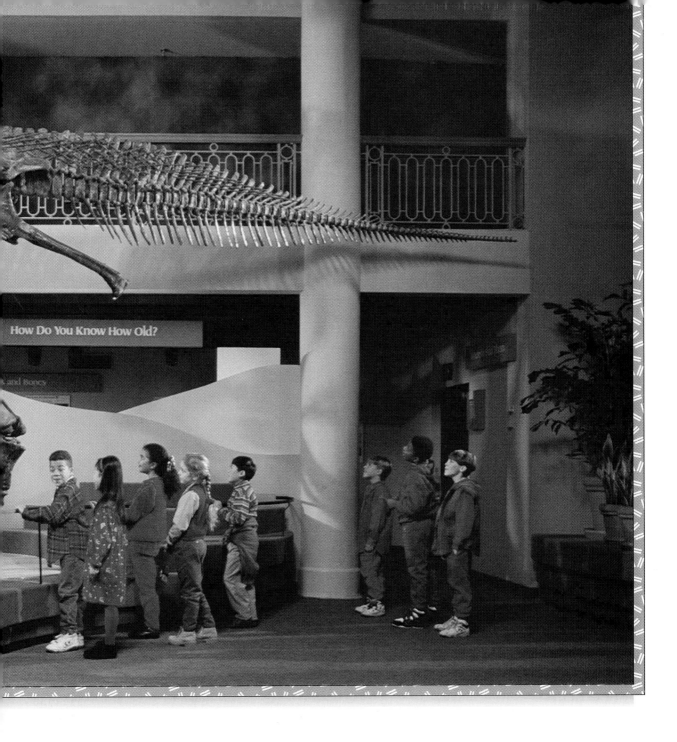

Imagine what scientists learn as they build skeletons. They don't only learn about a dinosaur's size and shape. They learn about other things as well.

Look at the skeleton of Corythosaurus. Its back legs are much larger than its front legs. What might this mean? It probably walked on two legs. Turn the page to see how this dinosaur might have looked.

An artist drew this picture. It shows how
Corythosaurus might have looked. What else can
you tell about this dinosaur?

Look at the head. It has a crest. The crest might
have been used to scare away other animals. It might
have been used to make sounds. What other clues
might skeletons give?

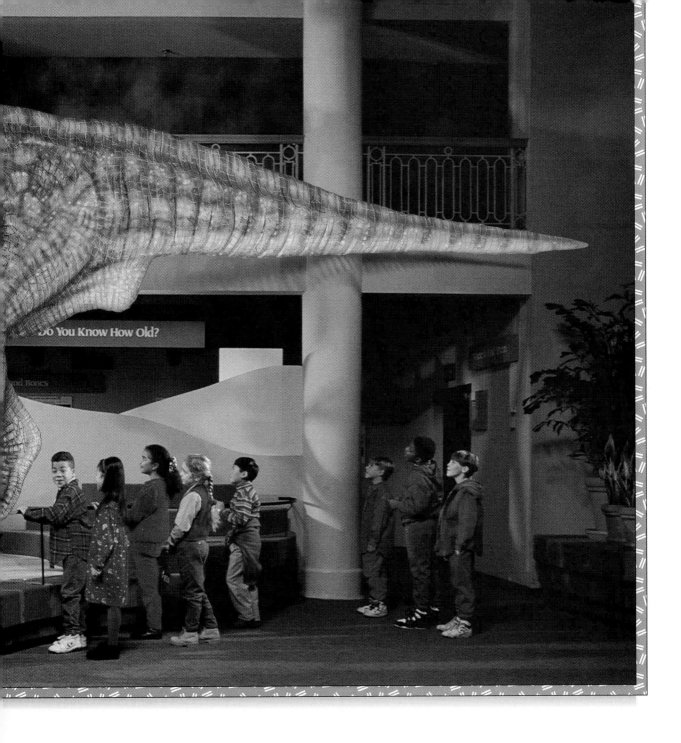

Scientists found a reptile with wings. It was covered with feathers. It might not have been able to fly. But it could climb. Scientists think that reptiles may be early relatives of birds.

Skeletons of whole families of dinosaurs have been found together. Scientists think this shows that some dinosaurs cared for their young.

Extinct and Endangered

Dinosaurs became **extinct** long ago. They can no longer be found on the earth. Yet some animals alive today are like dinosaurs. Some dinosaurs used beaks and claws to tear their food. Owls do that. Many dinosaur footprints were found in one place. This may mean that dinosaurs lived in herds. Cattle live in herds.

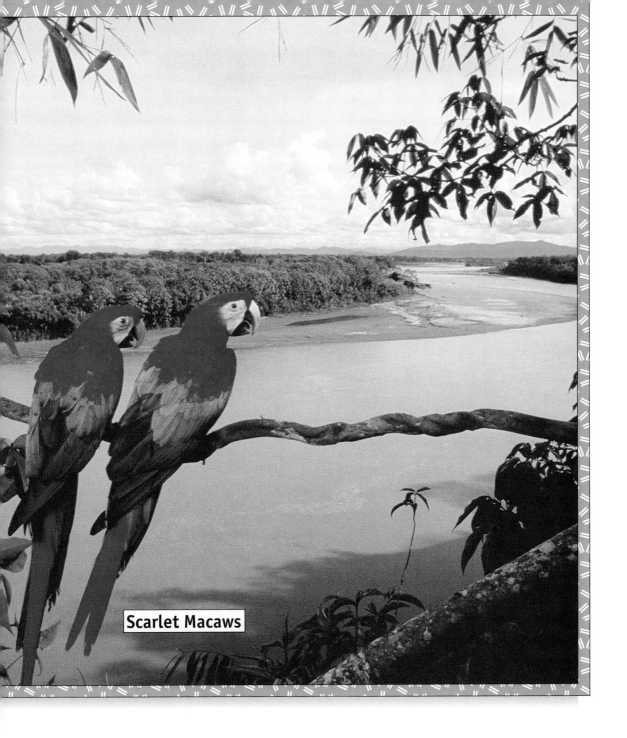

Scarlet Macaws

   Some animals today are as fun to learn about as dinosaurs. Yet many are in danger of no longer existing. The birds shown are **endangered**. How can you help animals like these? You can help save the places where they live. You can also help save the places where they get food. Let's keep these and other animals from becoming extinct.

Word Power

A. Match the words with a picture.
fossil imprint   fossil remains

a.

b.

B. Use these words to fill in the blanks.
dinosaurs   skeleton   endangered   fossils
flat teeth   pointed teeth   extinct   skull

1. You look at a dinosaur's _____ to see its teeth.
2. Animals that have _____ can tear food.
3. The bones of an animal make up its _____.
4. Millions of years ago, _____ lived on the earth.
5. Animals that have _____ can grind food.
6. Animals that are in danger of no longer existing
   are _____.
7. The remains or imprints of once-living things are
   called _____.
8. Animals that can no longer be found on the earth
   are _____.

Using Science Ideas

What two things can you tell about this dinosaur by looking at its skeleton?

Solving Science Problems

1. How can you tell if a fossil is remains or an imprint?

2. What are two ways that scientists get clues about dinosaurs?

3. What can you do to help endangered animals from becoming extinct?

UNIT D

SOLIDS, LIQUIDS, AND GASES

Theme: Constancy and Change

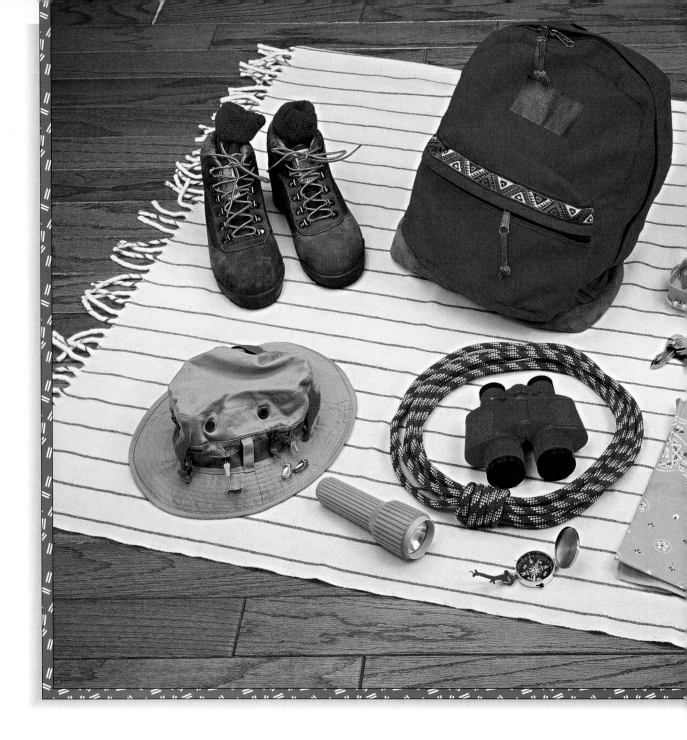

All About Solids

How are the objects in the picture alike? They are made of **matter**. They are solids. A **solid** does not change shape or size when it is moved.

You can describe a solid by its color, shape, size, and texture. The plate is blue and round. It is larger than the cup but smaller than the hat.

SOLIDS, LIQUIDS, AND GASES

The **texture** of an object describes how it feels
when you touch it. The plate feels smooth.

You can use color, shape, size, or texture to group
solids. The plate, the cup, and the coffeepot are all
blue objects. The log and the rope have rough
textures. Which would you group together by shape?
Which would you group by size?

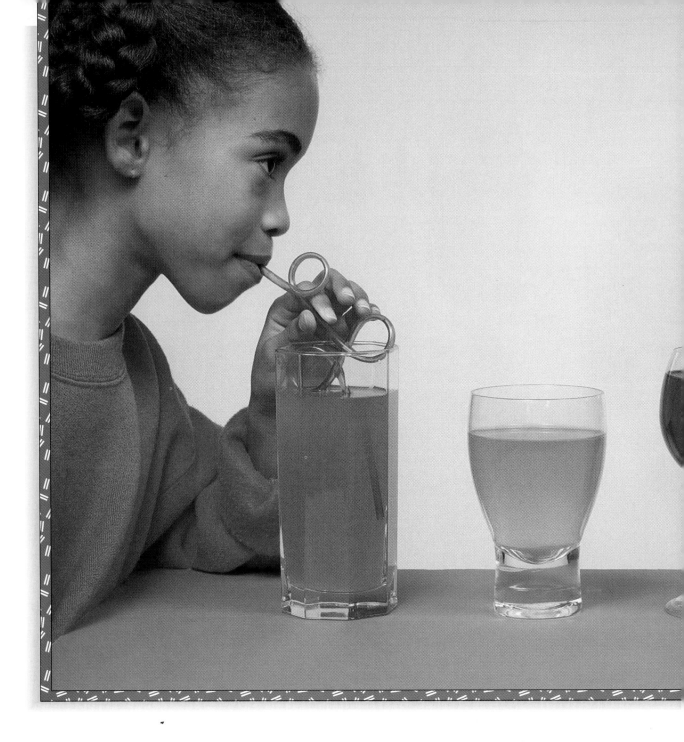

All About Liquids

Do you like to drink liquids? A **liquid** is matter that
changes shape when it is moved to another container.
Each liquid takes the shape of the glass it is in. If you
pour a liquid from a tall glass into one that is short and
wide, the liquid will take the shape of the short glass.
The liquid still takes up the same amount of space.

SOLIDS, LIQUIDS, AND GASES

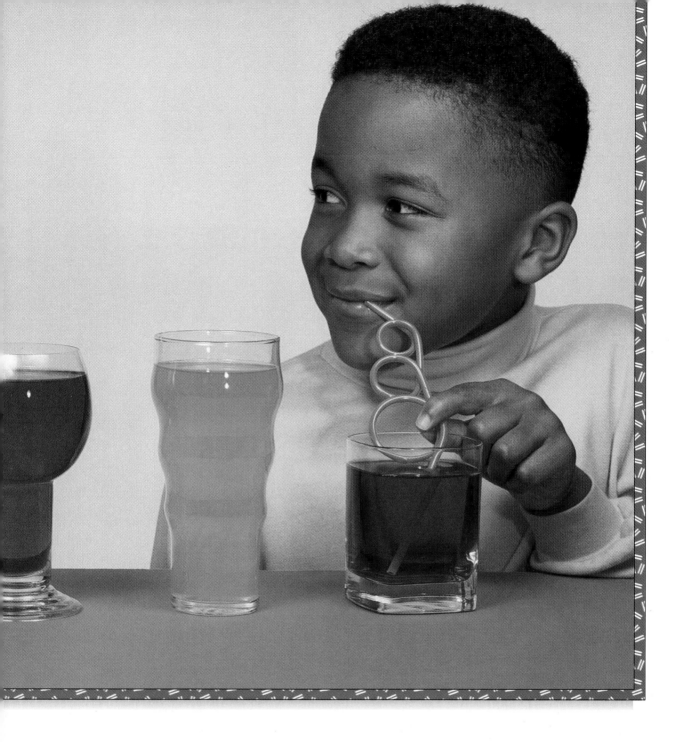

How can you describe a liquid? One way is by its color. Milk and grape juice are liquids of different colors. Milk is white. Grape juice is purple. What colors are some other liquids?

A liquid can also be described by its texture. Cooking oil feels slippery. Other liquids feel smooth or sticky. What liquids have felt sticky to you?

Looking at Shapes

You know that a solid has a definite shape. You also know that a liquid does not. A liquid takes the shape of the container it is in. You can use what you know to tell if something is a solid or a liquid.

Look at the picture. What is in each container? Does each container have a solid or a liquid in it?

SOLIDS, LIQUIDS, AND GASES

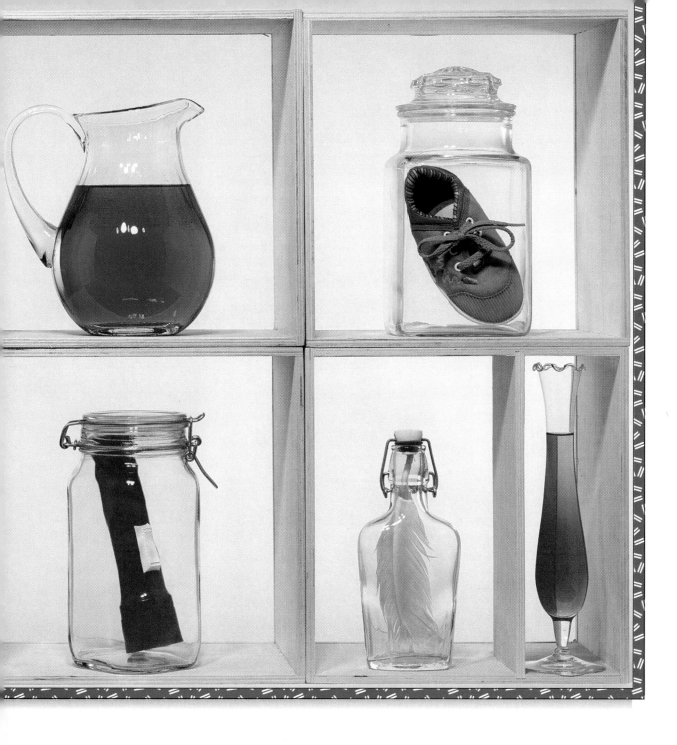

Is the flashlight a solid or a liquid? It is a solid because it has a definite shape. It does not take the shape of its container. If you put the flashlight into another container, it won't change shape.

Does the pitcher with blue matter in it hold a solid or a liquid? It holds a liquid. You can tell because the matter takes the shape of the container it is in.

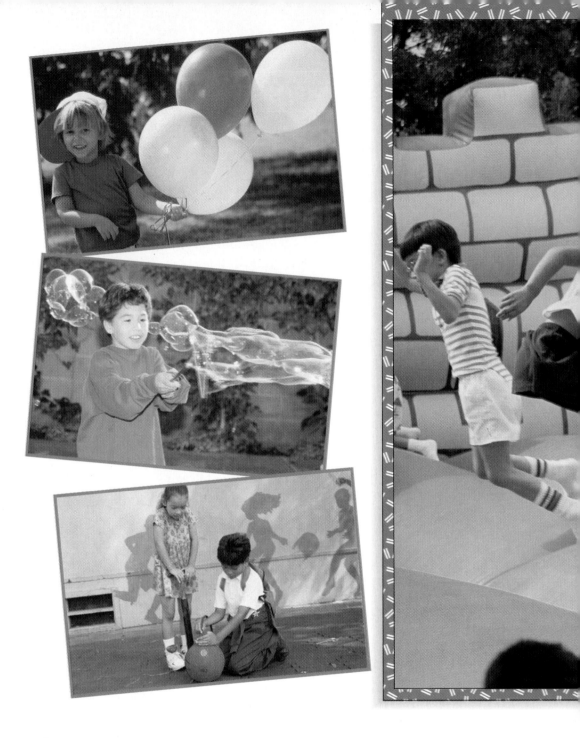

All About Gases

Gas is matter that is all around you and fills many kinds of things. Look at the pictures. There are gases in the balloons, the bubbles, and the ball. Gases fill the walls and floor of the funhouse.

Air is a gas that is all around the children. Air is all around you right now. You cannot see a gas.

A gas does not have a set shape. A gas fills a container and takes its shape. A gas can also change the shape of some containers. As gas is added to a balloon, the balloon changes shape.

Not all containers change shape when a gas is added. Think about blowing air into a glass jar. The jar does not change shape.

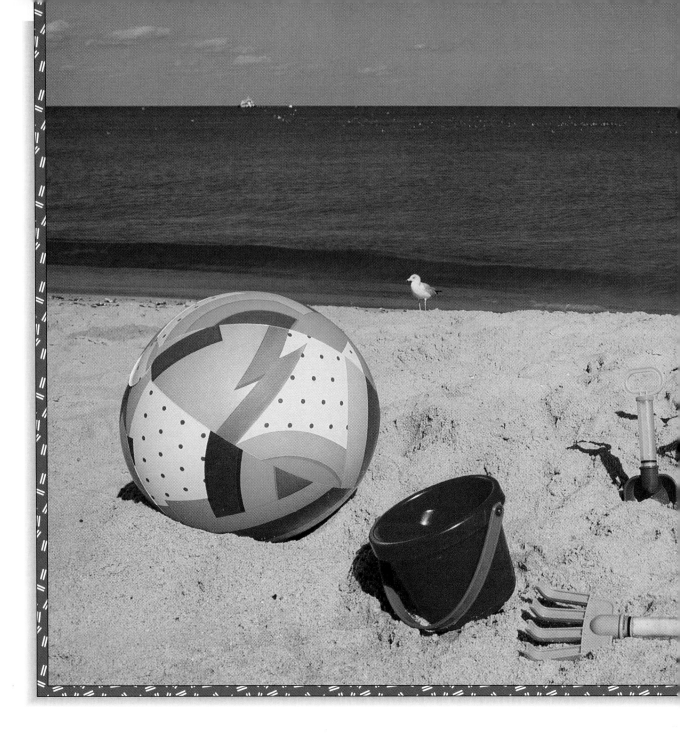

Taking Up Space

Look at this beach picture. The chair, the ball, the toys, the drink holder, and the sand are all solids. The ocean and the juice inside the drink holder are liquids.

You cannot see the gases in the picture. The ball is filled with gas. The air, which is all around everything in the picture, is a gas.

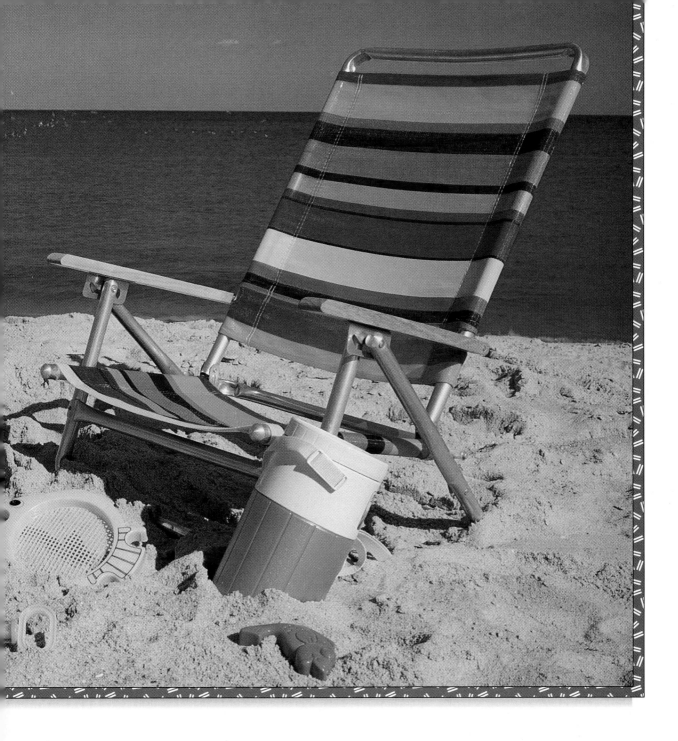

All objects—solids, liquids, and gases—are made of matter. All matter takes up space. Think about which object in the picture takes up the largest space. The ocean might be your choice. Or maybe you think it's the air or the beach.

Now think about which matter takes up the smallest space. Maybe it's one tiny grain of sand.

Solids Change to Liquids

Are these objects solids, liquids, or gases? They are solids. Think of ways you can describe their color, shape, size, and texture. There are yellow bananas, lemons, and ice pops. The blueberries, oranges, and limes are round. The raspberries and blueberries are small. The ice pops and bananas are smooth.

SOLIDS, LIQUIDS, AND GASES

What are the ice pops made of? You probably know they are made of ice. Ice is the solid form of water. Think of what you know about ice. What can happen to ice on a lake when the sun heats it?

Heat can make solid matter change form. What will happen to the solid ice pops if heat is added to them? Turn the page to find out.

How have the ice pops changed? They have melted. The air around the ice pops was warm. This **heat** made the solid ice pops change form.

Parts of some ice pops are not yet melted. What will happen if the ice pops stay in the warm air? All of the ice pops will probably melt.

The melted ice pops have taken the shape of their plates. How is this a clue that the solid ice pops have become liquid?

You know that ice is the solid form of water. When ice is heated, it changes to liquid water. Where should you keep an ice pop if you do not want it to melt?

Liquids Change to Gases

Cooling off in water can be fun. The children in the picture are spraying each other with water from a hose. What are some other ways you use water?

What can these children do to get dry if they do not have a towel? They can dry in the sun. They might run around and let the air dry them.

Where does the water go when children dry in the sun? The liquid water on the children's skin changes from a liquid to a gas. The gas is called **water vapor.** You cannot see water vapor.

A liquid **evaporates** when it changes to a gas. How do you feel when water evaporates from your skin? You usually feel cooler and drier.

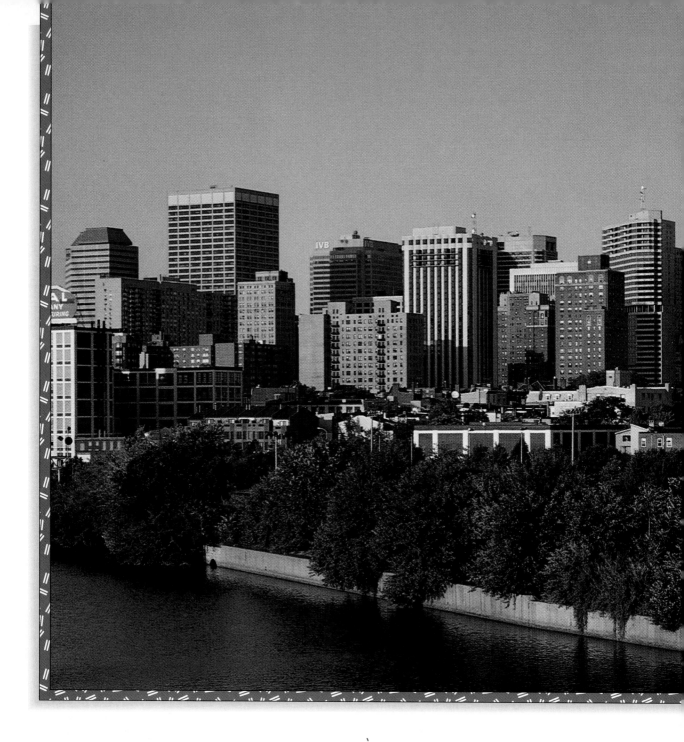

Gases Change to Liquids

You know that there is air all around. Air is a gas that you can't see. Water vapor is another gas. You can't see it. There is water vapor in the air.

Where does the water vapor in air come from? Water vapor forms when water evaporates. Look at the picture. Where might water vapor come from?

Water from the river warms. It evaporates and changes to water vapor. The water vapor rises into the air. As it rises, the water vapor in air becomes cooler and cooler.

When water vapor becomes cool enough, it changes to liquid water. A gas **condenses** when it changes to a liquid.

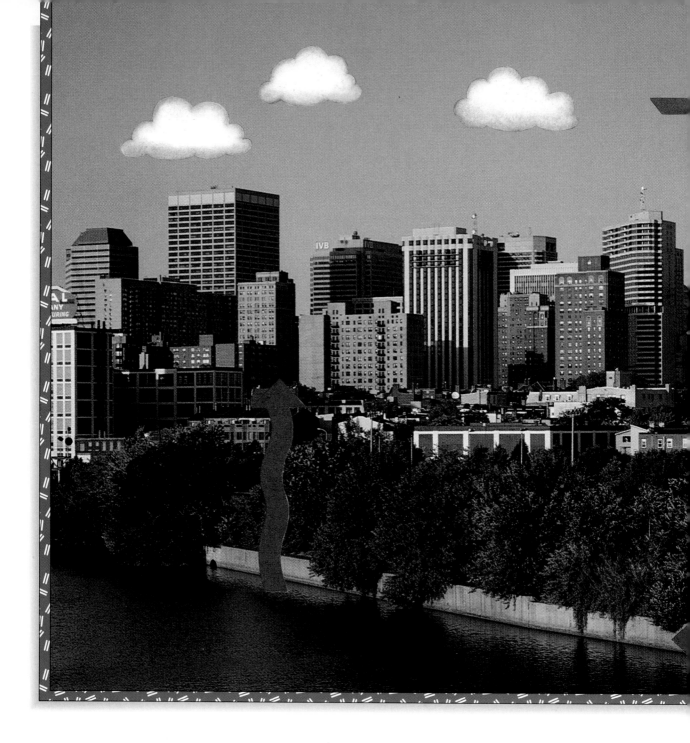

Look what has been added to this picture. Find the
arrow that points up from the river. It is wavy. This arrow
shows water evaporating from the river. Follow the arrow
to the sky. What do you see above the buildings?

As water vapor rises, it cools. The water vapor
condenses into tiny water drops. The tiny drops of
liquid water in the air form clouds.

Sometimes the tiny water drops in clouds form larger drops. Large and heavy drops fall as rain. Where does rain fall?

Water evaporates from the river. It condenses and forms clouds. The water in clouds falls back to the earth. Some of the water evaporates again. These changes in water are called the **water cycle.**

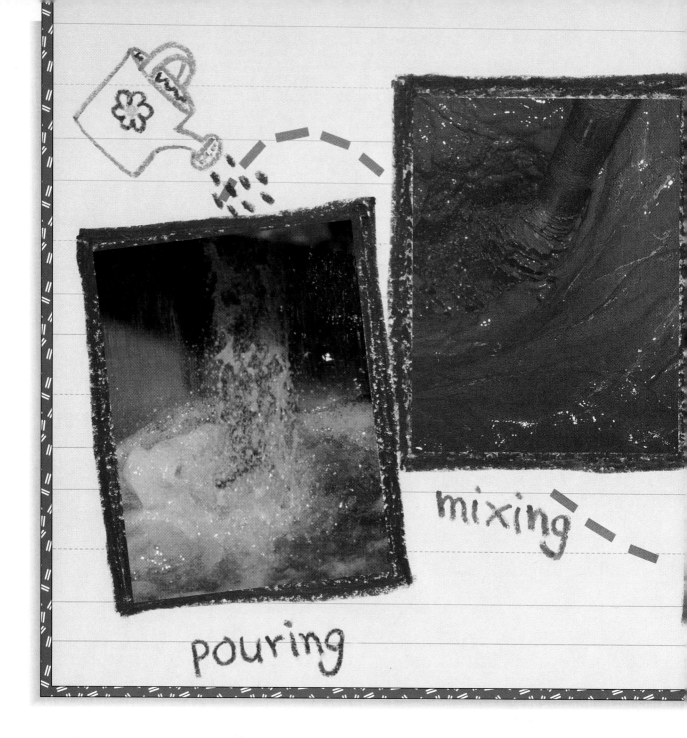

pouring

mixing

Liquids Change to Solids

Many things were once a different kind of matter than they are now. The pictures show the steps in making crayons. Look at the first picture. It shows liquid wax. Wax was heated to make it **melt.**

Now look at the second picture. It shows color being mixed into the liquid wax.

moving along

sorting

Look at the last two pictures. Here the crayons have changed from liquid to solid. The liquid wax is poured into molds shaped like crayons. As it cools, the liquid changes to a solid.

A liquid **freezes** when it changes to a solid. Juice can become an ice pop when it cools enough to freeze. What other liquids freeze into useful solids?

Matter Everywhere

Matter is all around you. A solid has a definite size. It also has a definite shape. A liquid has a definite amount. It does not have a definite shape. Gases have no definite size or shape.

Look at the picture. Find solids, liquids, and gases. The next page gives you some examples. Can you find more?

SOLIDS, LIQUIDS, AND GASES

Solids   The buildings, the plants, the signs, the stove, and the bathtub are some of the solids.

Liquids   The milk in the baby's bottle, the water in the bathtub and sink, the bubble liquid, and the drops that make up the clouds are liquids.

Gases   The balloons, the blimp, the bubbles, and the ball have gas in them.

Word Power

A. Match the words with a picture.

solid   liquid   gas

a.   b.   c.

B. Use these words to fill in the blanks.

matter   water vapor   heat   evaporates
freezes   condenses   texture   melts

1. All objects are made of _____.
2. When a liquid changes to a solid, it _____.
3. When a liquid changes to a gas, it _____.
4. When a gas changes to a liquid, it _____.
5. How something feels is its _____.
6. When a solid changes to a liquid, it _____.
7. When water is a gas, it is called _____.
8. Energy that can change a solid to a liquid is called _____.

Using Science Ideas

How many solids, liquids, and gases can you find in the picture? List them.

Solving Science Problems

1. Why do crayons melt in a hot car?

2. Describe one way that matter changes form.

3. Make a chart like the one shown. Add more objects to your chart. Put checks in the right places.

Object	Has its own shape	Takes the shape of its container	Spreads out to fill its container	Kind of matter
doll	✔			solid

UNIT E

WHAT MAKES ME SICK

Themes: Systems, Scale

Looking at Germs

Germs can get inside your body. They can make you sick. Bacteria and viruses are two kinds of germs. You need to use a **microscope** to see bacteria. Viruses are too small to be seen. You can't see them with a microscope. Look at the picture. It shows what bacteria look like under a microscope.

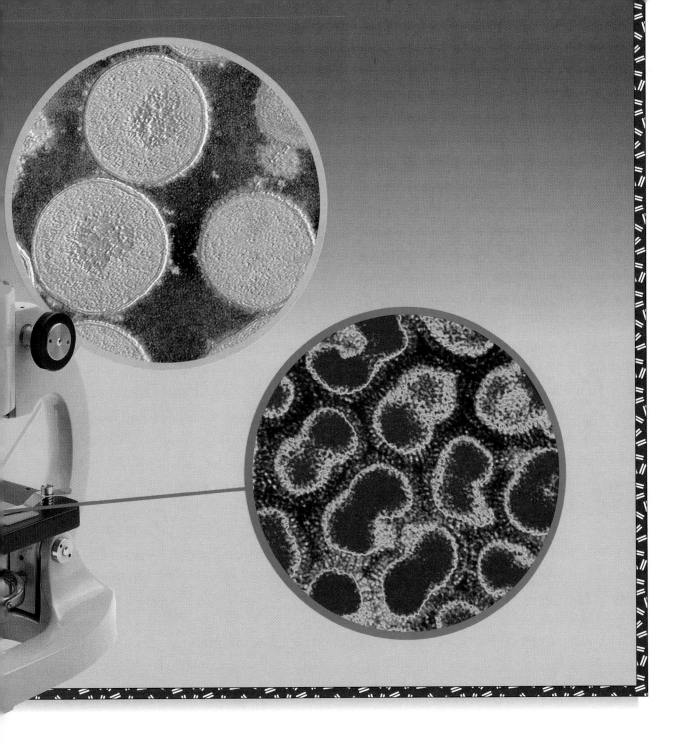

Different germs cause different sicknesses. Two kinds of **viruses** cause colds and chickenpox. **Bacteria** cause some kinds of sore throats. Have you ever had a sickness caused by germs?

Do you know why you should learn about germs? Knowing about germs is one way you can help yourself and others stay healthy.

Sneezing Spreads Germs

The picture shows a boy sneezing. It begins with the boy throwing back his head. It ends with the boy sneezing into his hands. As he **sneezes**, air and liquid come out of his nose and mouth. There are germs in the liquid. The large circle shows how these germs look under a microscope.

What are some ways to keep germs from spreading when you sneeze? You can cover your nose and mouth with your hands as the boy in the picture is doing.

You can also hold a tissue over your nose and mouth. Then you should put the tissue in the trash. You should use soap and water to wash the germs off your hands.

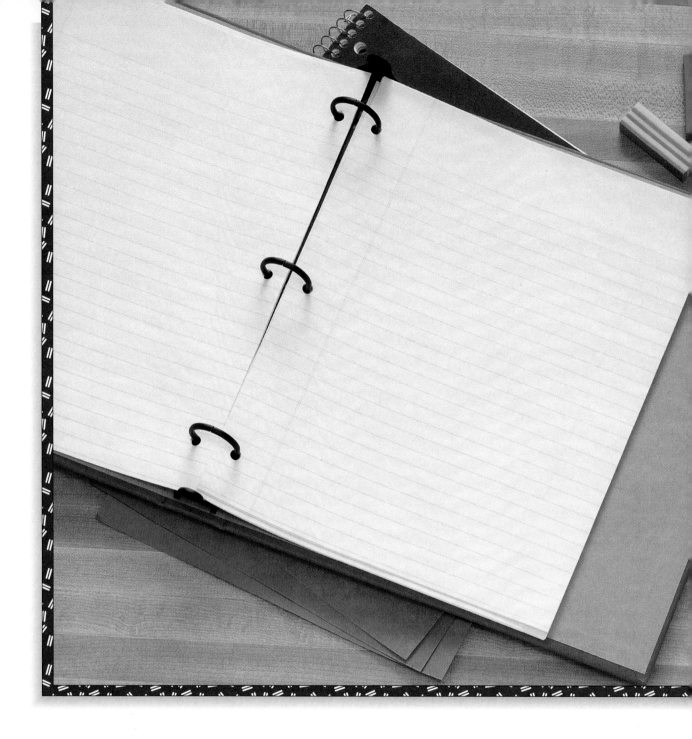

Germs Everywhere

Look at the picture. Think about places where you might find germs. There are germs everywhere. All the objects—the books, notebooks, pencils, scissors, paper clips, erasers, and table—have germs on them. Germs are very small. Even though you cannot see germs, you know they are there.

How do you think germs spread to the objects in the picture? Some germs come from the hands of people who touch the objects.

People may sneeze near the objects. If they do not cover their noses and mouths, germs get on the objects. Then when someone picks up one of the objects, germs **spread** to his or her hands.

This picture shows some of the germs that could be on the objects. These germs are shown just as you would see them under a microscope.

Arrows point to places where the germs might be. It looks like there are a lot of germs in the circles. There are really many more. Remember, germs are very small.

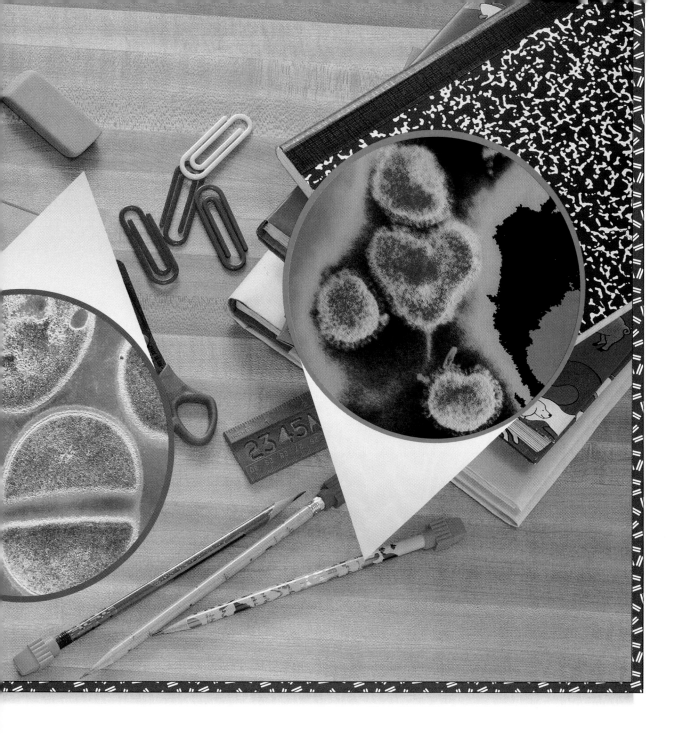

What are some ways you can keep germs from spreading? You can wash the desk. You can wash your hands. You can decide not to share books, pencils, and erasers. You can cover your nose and mouth with a tissue when you sneeze. You can also keep things that don't normally go in your mouth out of your mouth.

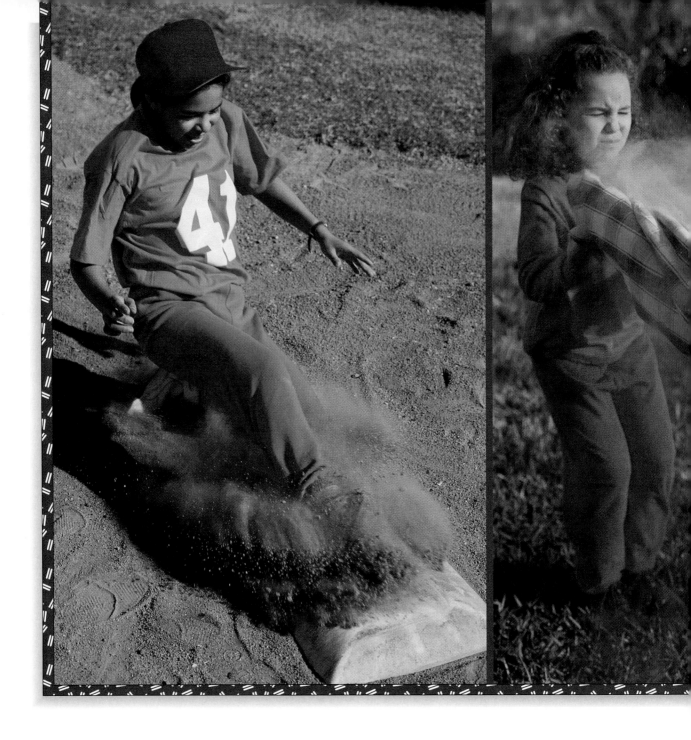

Trapping Germs

Look at the picture of the girl playing baseball. She is kicking up dust as she slides. What are the other children doing? They are also putting dust into the air.

Think about how it feels to breathe with dust in the air. Dust can make it hard to breathe. Dust has germs in it. So dust puts germs into the air.

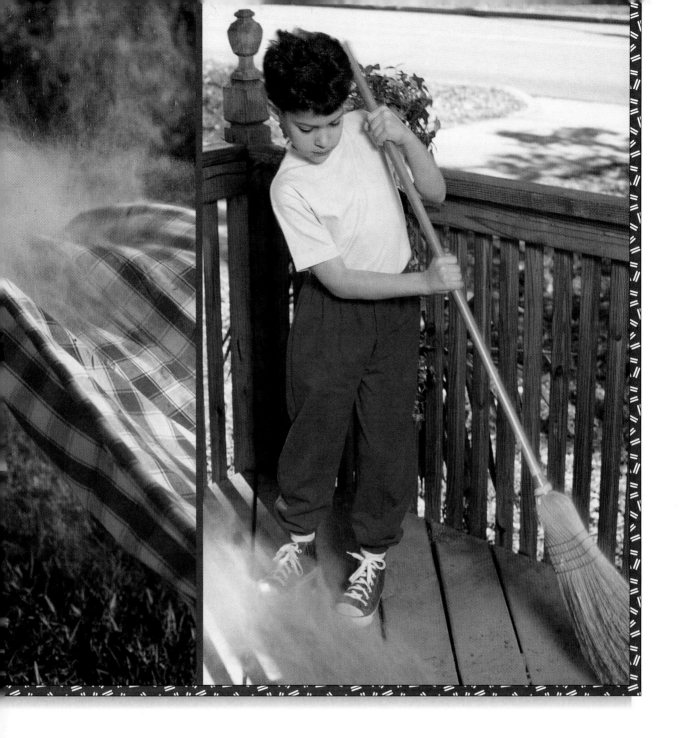

What are some ways your body protects you from germs? One way is by trapping dust and germs in mucus. **Mucus** is a sticky material in your nose, mouth, and throat.

Mucus helps trap dust and germs to keep them from getting further into your body. Germs cannot make you sick if they cannot get into your body.

Protect Yourself

Think about how germs might be spread in each picture. The first boy has cut his knee. Germs can get inside his body through the cut. The girls are drinking from the same straw. They are sharing germs. The last boy is about to pick up an apple core. It has on it the germs of the person that ate it.

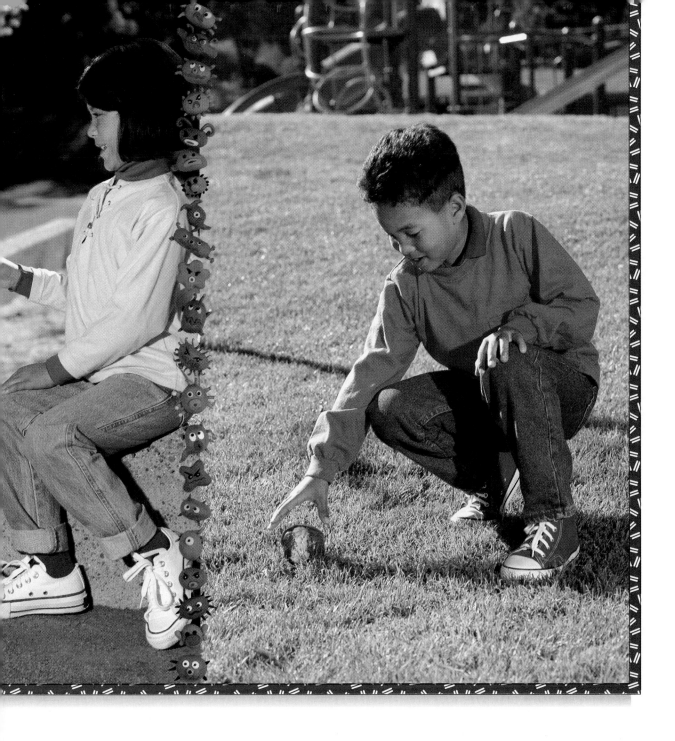

What can be done to keep germs from spreading?
The first boy can wash the cut with soap and water.
Then he can put a bandage on it to keep it clean. Each
girl should have her own drink.

The last boy should use a napkin or paper towel to
pick up the apple core and throw it away. Then he
should wash his hands with soap and water.

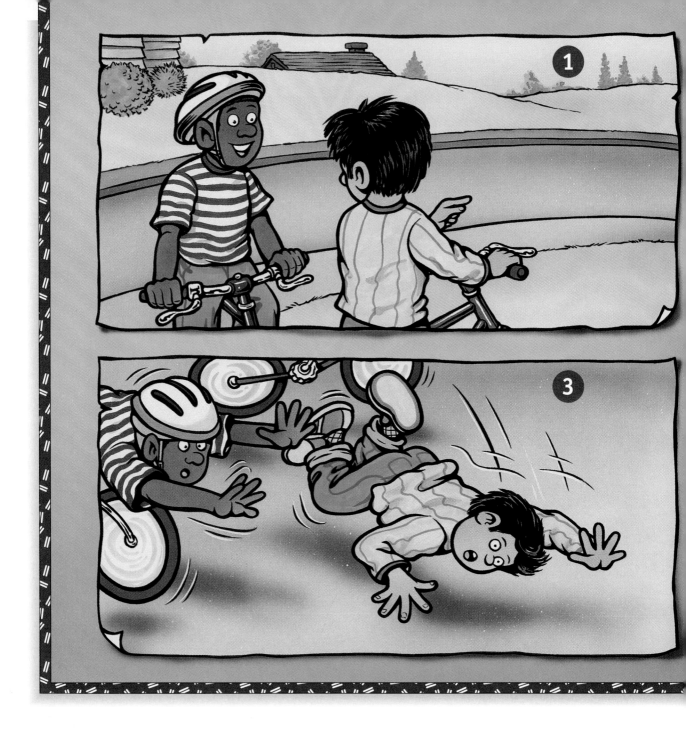

Preventing Injury

Look at the picture story. What happened? One of the boys hit his head on the sidewalk. He has an **injury**. Why does one boy have an injury but the other boy does not? The boy that hurt his head was not wearing a safety helmet. The boy without the injury was wearing a safety helmet.

WHAT MAKES ME SICK

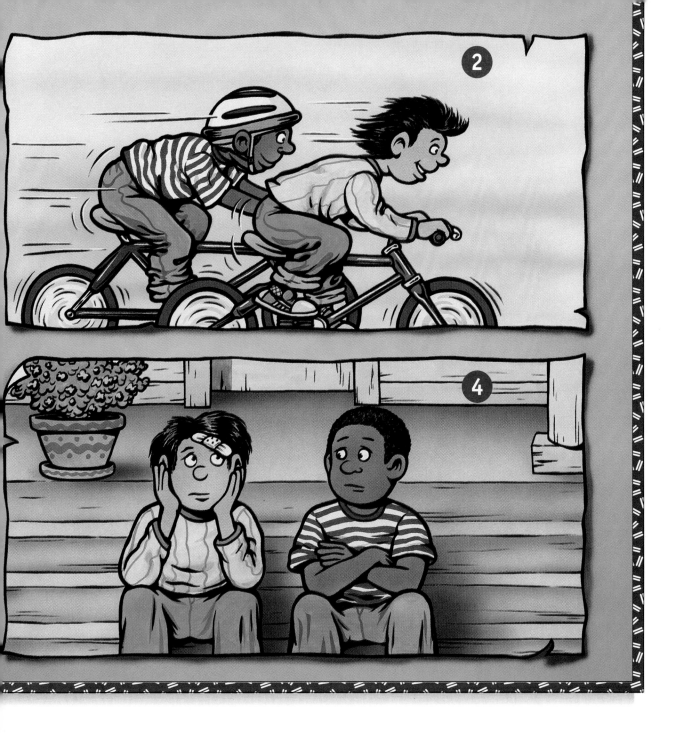

The boy who hurt his head can **prevent**, or stop, an injury from happening again. He can wear a safety helmet. What else can the boy do to prevent an injury?

The boy can pedal slower. He can be careful to watch where he is going. The boy might even decide to wear elbow pads on his arms and knee pads on his legs.

Staying Healthy

What are some ways you can keep your body healthy? You can eat healthful foods. These kinds of foods help your body grow strong. You can also exercise. This will make your muscles and bones stronger.

Getting enough sleep helps keep you healthy, too. When you sleep, your body gets the rest it needs.

What are some things that are not good for your body? Too many cookies, candies, or potato chips are not good for you. Alcohol, cigarettes, and drugs are not good for you, either.

Follow the maze with your finger. Decide which things are good for your body. You will get to the finish by choosing healthful things.

Word Power

A. Match the words with a picture.
microscope   germs

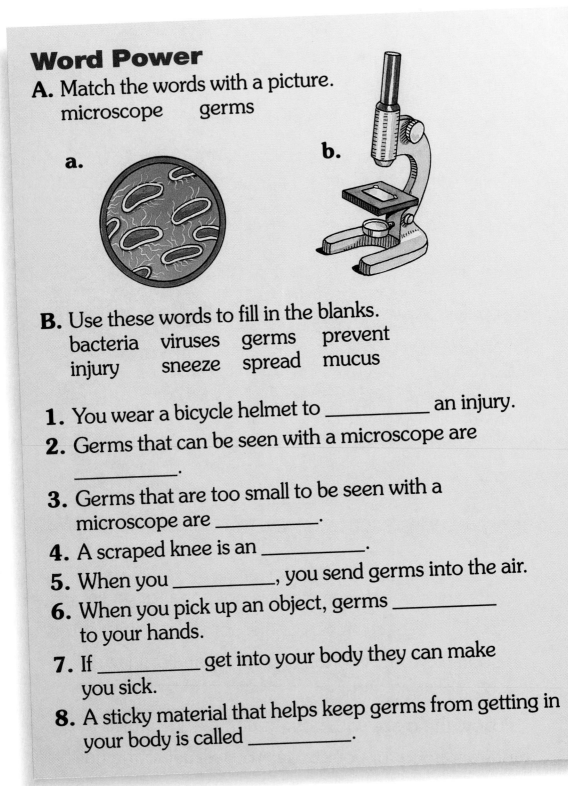

a.

b.

B. Use these words to fill in the blanks.
bacteria   viruses   germs   prevent
injury   sneeze   spread   mucus

1. You wear a bicycle helmet to _____ an injury.

2. Germs that can be seen with a microscope are _____.

3. Germs that are too small to be seen with a microscope are _____.

4. A scraped knee is an _____.

5. When you _____, you send germs into the air.

6. When you pick up an object, germs _____ to your hands.

7. If _____ get into your body they can make you sick.

8. A sticky material that helps keep germs from getting in your body is called _____.

Using Science Ideas

How are germs being spread? Make a list.

Solving Science Problems

1. Describe two ways that you can help germs from spreading to others when you are sick.

2. How does the body protect itself from germs?

3. Make a chart like the one shown. List activities and things that you can do to stay healthy. Add your own ideas to the chart.

Activities	Staying Healthy
Bike riding	Wear a bicycle helmet
Roller skating	
Sneezing	

GLOSSARY

B

bacteria Tiny living things that can only be seen with a microscope. Some bacteria cause sickness. (E3)

beak The jaws of a bird along with their hard coverings. A bird uses its beak to pick up food. Beaks are also called bills. (A14)

beam A ray of light. A laser produces a narrow beam of light. (B10)

C

condense To change from a gas to a liquid. When water vapor in the air cools, it condenses to form clouds. (D19)

D

dinosaur An animal that lived millions of years ago. All dinosaurs lived on land. (C2)

E

endangered A living thing that may become extinct. The giant panda is an endangered animal. (C23)

erosion The washing away of the land. The roots of trees can help stop erosion. (A21)

evaporate To change from a liquid to a gas. Water evaporates to form water vapor. (D17)

extinct When all animals of one kind die. There are no dinosaurs today because these animals are extinct. (C22)

flat teeth Teeth that are good for grinding food. Many plant-eating dinosaurs had flat teeth. (C14)

fossil imprint A mark formed when a plant or animal leaves a trace, or print, of itself in soil, which gradually turns to rock. (C8)

fossil remains What is left of a plant or animal that lived long ago. (C12)

fossil Remain or imprint of a once-living thing. Dinosaur footprints in rock are one kind of fossil. (C6)

freeze To change from a liquid to a solid. Water freezes into ice when the temperature is below 32°F. (D23)

gas A form of matter that does not have a set shape. A gas spreads out to fill what it is in. (D8)

germ A tiny living thing that can make you sick. (E2)

habitat A place in which a plant or animal lives. In its habitat a living thing gets all the things it needs. (A4)

heat A form of energy used to change matter. Heat is used to warm homes. Heat can change a solid to a liquid. (B8, D14)

injury Something harmful that happens to a person. Some injuries are cuts, scrapes, bruises, and broken bones. (E14)

leaves Parts of a plant that grow on a stem or grow up from roots. Leaves make food. (A7)

light A form of energy that you can see. The sun and the stars give off light. (B2)

liquid Matter that takes the shape of its container. (D4)

living thing Something that is alive. Living things move, need food, and grow. (A2)

lodge A beaver's home. (A18)

matter What all things are made of. All matter takes up space. (D2)

melt To change from a solid to a liquid. When ice melts, it changes to liquid water. (D22)

microscope A tool that makes small things appear larger. Bacteria can be seen with the aid of a microscope. (E2)

mucus A sticky material that traps germs and dust. It prevents these things from reaching the lungs. (E11)

nonliving thing Something that was never alive. A rock is a nonliving thing. (A3)

once-living thing Something that was alive at one time or was once part of a living thing. Logs used to make a fence are examples of once-living things. (A3)

opaque A material that keeps light from passing through. An opaque object casts a shadow. The human body and a paper bag are both opaque. (B12)

pointed teeth Sharp teeth that are good for tearing food. Many meat-eating dinosaurs had pointed teeth. (C14)

prevent To keep from happening. Wearing a helmet when skating can help prevent injury. (E15)

prism A clear object shaped like a pyramid. A prism bends light and separates it into the colors of the rainbow. (B23)

rainbow Made when drops of water in the sky act like prisms and break the sunlight into colors. The colors of the rainbow are red, orange, yellow, green, blue, indigo, and violet. (B22)

reflect To throw back. The moon reflects the light of the sun. (B7)

remains Fossils that were part of the real animal. Fossil bones are remains. (C6)

resource Anything that plants or animals use to live. (A11)

root The part of a plant that grows down into the soil. Roots hold the plant in place, soak up water, and sometimes store food. (A6)

shadow A dark shape formed when an object blocks light. Shadows can become longer or shorter. (B16)

shelter A place where an animal can rest and be safe. An animal stores food and raises its young in a shelter. (A12)

skeleton The bones of the body that hold up the body and help it move. Scientists have found dinosaur skeletons. (C18)

skull The bone that shapes your head and protects your brain. (C16)

sneeze A sudden forcing of breath through the nose and mouth. Sneezing is one way that germs are spread. (E4)

solid A form of matter that has its own shape. When a solid is put into a jar, the shape of the solid stays the same. (D2)

spine The tiny, sharp leaves of a cactus. Spines protect the plant from being eaten by animals. (A7)

spread To pass from one person to another. Diseases are spread by sneezing, coughing, and touching objects that have germs on them. (E7)

stem The supporting and connecting part of a plant. Water and food move through stems. (A6)

straight Not bent or curved. Light travels in a straight line. (B11)

texture The way something feels. Rough and smooth are textures. (D3)

translucent Allowing some light to pass through. Some translucent objects are frosted glass and waxed paper. (B12)

transparent Allowing light to pass through. Clear water and plastic wrap are transparent. (B12)

virus A very small germ that causes sickness. Viruses are too small to be seen, even with a microscope. (E3)

water cycle The changes that happen to water in nature. The steps of the water cycle are (1) water evaporates, (2) water condenses to form clouds, (3) water falls as rain, (4) water evaporates again. (D21)

water vapor Water that is a gas. You cannot see water vapor. (D17)

SAYING DINOSAUR NAMES

Albertosaurus al bur tuh SAWR us

Allosaurus al oh SAWR us

Ankylosaurus ang kuh loh SAWR us

Brachiosaurus brak *ee* uh SAWR us

Compsognathus kahmp SAHG nuh thus

Corythosaurus kawr ihnth uh SAWR us

Diplodocus dih PLAHD uh kus

Edmontosaurus ed mahn tuh SAWR us

Lambeosaurus lam bee oh SAWR us

Ornitholestes awr nih thuh LES teez

Ouranosaurus uh rahn uh SAWR us

Seismosaurus syz muh SAWR us

Stenonychosaurus sten oh nyk uh SAWR us

Triceratops trye SER uh tahps

Tyrannosaurus tuh ran uh SAWR us

Velociraptor vuh LAHS uh rap tur

INDEX

CREDITS

Cover: *Photography:* Jade Albert; *Photography Production:* Picture It Corporation; *Illustration:* Doreen Gay-Kassel.

ILLUSTRATORS
UNIT A A8–A9: Robert Roper. **A12–A13:** Debbie Pinkney Davis. **A16–A19:** Bob Pepper. **A20–A21:** Jenny Campbell. **A26:** Tom Pansini.

UNIT B B2–B3: Katie Keller. **B4–B7:** Ron Young. **B8–B9:** Jackie Urbanovic. **B16–B19:** Peggy Tagel. **B24–B27:** Eugenie Fernandes. **B28:** Tom Pansini.

UNIT C C2–C3: Richard Courtney. **C4–C5:** Phil Wilson. **C10–C11:** *t.* Taylor Oughton; *b.* Ka Botzis. **C12–C13:** Mike Meaker. **C14–C17:** Phil Wilson. **C20–C21:** Phil Wilson. **C24:** Tom Pansini.

UNIT D D20–D21: Carolyn Croll. **D24–D25:** Brian Karas. **D26:** Tom Pansini.

UNIT E E14–E15: Jerry Zimmerman. **E12–E13:** Doreen Gay-Kassel **E16–E17:** Jenny Campbell. **E18–E19:** Tom Pansini.

GLOSSARY: Tom Pansini.

PHOTOGRAPHS
All photographs by Silver Burdett Ginn (SBG) unless otherwise noted.

UNIT A A2–A3: Randy Wells/Allstock/Tony Stone Images. **A4:** Laurence Hughes/The Image Bank. **A5:** Pat O'Hara/Allstock/Tony Stone Images. **A6–A9:** Runk/Schoenberger/Grant Heilman Photography. **A10–A11:** James Randklev/Allstock/Tony Stone Images. **A14–A15:** *t.l.* © Francis Gohier/Photo Researchers, Inc.; *t.m.* William J. Weber/Visuals Unlimited; *t.r.* Darrell Gulin/Allstock/Tony Stone Images; *b.l., b.r.* ZEFA Germany/The Stock Market; *b.m.* Tom Tietz/Tony Stone Images. **A16, A18:** *t.l.* © Pat & Tom Leeson/Photo Researchers, Inc.; *m.l.* Tom Mangelson/Images of Nature; *b.l.* Johnny Johnson/Animals Animals. **A22–A23:** Gabe Palmer/The Stock Market. **A24:** Tony Stone Images. **A25:** Charles Kreb/Allstock. **A27:** Erwin & Peggy Bauer/Bruce Coleman, Inc.

UNIT B B10–B11: Peter Fox for SBG. **B12–B15:** Superstock. **B20–B21:** Peter Fox for SBG. **B22–B23:** G. Nagele/FPG International.

UNIT C C6: Courtesy, Peter Gregg. **C6–C7:** Jim Richardson/Westlight. **C8:** Breck P. Kent. **C8–C9:** Tom Bean. **C18–C21:** Mike Peters for SBG. **C22–C23:** Frans Lanting/Minden Pictures. **C25:** Louis Psihoyos/Matrix International, Inc.

UNIT D D8: *t.l.* B. Taylor/H. Armstrong Roberts; *m.l.* Tony Freeman/PhotoEdit; *b.l.* Michael Newman/PhotoEdit. **D8–D9:** Shelly Boyd/PhotoEdit. **D16–D17:** Tom McCarthy/PhotoEdit. **D18–D21:** Martin Rogers/Stock Boston. **D22–D23:** Oz Charles.

UNIT E E2: *t.* © Michael Abbey/Photo Researchers, Inc; *b.* © Biophoto Associates/Science Source/Photo Researchers, Inc. **E3:** *t.* © CNRI/Science Photo Library/Photo Researchers, Inc; *b.* © CDC/Science Source/Photo Researchers, Inc. **E4–E5:** Globus Studios for SBG. **E5:** © P. Hawtin, University of Southampton/Science Photo Library/Photo Researchers, Inc. **E8:** © David Phillips/Photo Researchers, Inc. **E8–E9:** © CNRI/Science Photo Library/Photo Researchers, Inc. **E9:** © NIBSC/Science Photo Library/Photo Researchers, Inc. **E10–E11:** David Phillips. **E12–E13:** Grant Huntington for SBG.